the REFORMATION

the REFORMATION

how a Monk and a Mallet Changed the World

STEPHEN J. NICHOLS

⁛ CROSSWAY®

WHEATON, ILLINOIS

Cover design: Jon McGrath

Cover photo: Art Resource Inc.

First printing, 2007

Printed in the United States of America

Illustrations on pages 19, 27,33, 36, 40, 42, 43, 70, 75, 81, 83, 96, 117, 132, 133, 140, 142, and 144 are used by courtesy of Montgomery Library, Westminster Theological Seminary.

Illustrations on pages 49, 61,62,65,66, and 137 are used by courtesy of Lancaster Mennonite Historical Society.

Illustration on page 74 is used by courtesy of the H. Henry Meeter Center for Calvin Studies.

Scripture quotations are taken from the ESV® Bible (*The Holy Bible: English Standard Version®*). Copyright © 2001 by Crossway. Used by permission. All rights reserved.

ISBN-13: 978-1-58134-829-3
ISBN-10: 1-58134-829-0
ePub ISBN: 978-1-4335-1961-1
PDF ISBN: 978-1-4335-0170-8
Mobipocket ISBN: 978-1-4335-0856-1

Library of Congress Cataloging-in-Publication Data
Nichols, Stephen J., 1970–
   The Reformation : how a monk and a mallet changed the world /
Stephen J. Nichols.
     p.   cm.
   Includes bibliographical references.
   ISBN 13: 978-1-58134-829-3 (tpb)
   ISBN 10: 1-58134-829-0
   1. Reformation. 2. Church history—16th century. I. Title.
BR305.3.N53   2007
270.6—dc22   2006024076

Crossway is a publishing ministry of Good News Publishers.

VP		26	25	24	23	22	21	20	19	18	17	16
21	20	19	18	17	16	15	14	13	12	11	10	9

For

LESTER HICKS

SEAN LUCAS

DALE MORT

in appreciation of your friendship

CONTENTS

Acknowledgments   9

List of Illustrations   10

Introduction   11

1   Five Hundred Years Old and Still Going Strong   13
    Why the Reformation Matters Today

2   A Monk and A Mallet   25
    Martin Luther and the German Reformation

3   Some Middle-Aged Men and a Sausage Supper   39
    Ulrich Zwingli and the Swiss Reformation

4   The Not-So-Radical Radical Reformers   55
    The Anabaptists and the Reformation

5   An Overnight Stay in Geneva   69
    John Calvin and the Swiss Reformation

6   A King and a Divorce   85
    The Anglicans and the British Reformation

7   Men in Black   99
    The Puritans and the British Reformation

8   Women in Black Too   115
    The Untold Story of Women and the Reformation

Appendix   129
    In Their Own Words: Selections from Documents of the Reformation

Notes   151

Almighty God, who through the preaching of thy servants, the blessed reformers, hast caused the light of the Gospel to shine forth: Grant, we beseech thee, that knowing its saving power, we may faithfully guard and defend it against all enemies, and joyfully proclaim it, to the salvation of souls and the glory of thy Holy Name; through thy Son, Jesus Christ our Lord, who liveth and reigneth with thee and the Holy Spirit, one God, world without end. Amen.

Prayer for Reformation Day, Lutheran Service Book & Hymnal

Almighty God and Father, grant unto us, because we have to go through much strife on this earth, the strength of thy Holy Spirit, in order that we may courageously go through the fire, and through the water, and that we may put ourselves so under thy rule that we may go to meet death in full confidence of thy assistance and without fear.

A prayer of John Calvin

ACKNOWLEDGMENTS

I am grateful to many who have contributed to this book. First, a grateful thanks to Steve Brown, Mike Horton, and Sinclair Ferguson for not only reading the manuscript but also finding something nice to say about it. A trio of friends also deserves mention. Sean Lucas deserves a deep word of thanks for continually honing my historical sensibilities. Dale Mort graciously read every word and was even more gracious in his suggestions for changes. Lester Hicks demonstrates again and again the value of friendship and collegiality. It is to these three friends that I dedicate this book. We're not quite a band of reformers, but we are trying.

I am deeply appreciative of those who assisted with illustrations, including Carolyn Wenger, Lancaster Mennonite Historical Society, and Melvin Hartwick, Montgomery Library, Westminister Theological Seminary. Diane Fisher, whose friendship and skills as a reference librarian are deeply appreciated, graciously volunteered her efforts for illustrations. Eric Brandt, upon whose talents I am relying more and more, helped in a number of ways, including setting up the book's web site.

Much of this material was worked out before some rather encouraging congregations and groups. I am grateful for the occasions provided by Westminster Presbyterian Church (Lancaster, Pennsylvania), Evangelical United Methodist Church (New Holland, Pennsylvania), and Pinebrook Bible Conference in the Pocono Mountains. These kind folks helped me think through the meaning of the Reformation for today. I am also grateful for the support and encouragement from my students, colleagues, and administrators at Lancaster Bible College.

The final chapter begins by noting the laudable wives of the Reformers. My wife, I can easily say, would rival any one of them. To Heidi I am grateful for everything.

LIST OF ILLUSTRATIONS

Jan Hus   19

Martin Luther   27

The Castle at Wartburg   32

Philip Melanchthon   33

English Edition of Luther's Psalms Commentary   36

Ulrich Zwingli   40

Erasmus's Greek New Testament, 1516   42

Erasmus of Rotterdam   43

Zurich   49

Menno Simons   61

Martyrdom of Maria von Monjou by Drowning, 1552   62

Thieleman J. van Braght   65

Secret Anabaptist Church Service, Amsterdam, 1560s   66

Acts of the Synod of Dort, 1620   70

Handwritten Manuscript of John Calvin   74

William Farel   75

Theodore Beza   81

Calvin's Commentary on New Testament Epistles, 1556   83

England's Kings and Queens Scorecard   87

Edward VI and Mary   88

John Knox   96

William Laud   102

Letter from Oliver Cromwell to John Cotton   103

London, 1647   111

Johannes Oecolampadius   117

Anne Bradstreet   125

Thomas Cranmer   132

John Calvin   133

Anabaptist Martyrdoms, Saltzburg, 1528   137

Ordinance by Parliament Calling for Westminster Assembly, 1643   140

Directory for Public Worship, 1644   142

Caspar Olevianus   144

Reformation Scorecard   158-159

INTRODUCTION

Historians like dates. And one of the dates that historians like best is October 31, 1517. On that day one monk with mallet in hand nailed a document to the church door in Wittenberg. It contained a list of Ninety-Five Theses for a debate. The immediate concern was an indulgence sale to finance St. Peter's Basilica in Rome and the Sistine Chapel—Michelangelo didn't come cheap. Martin Luther, the mallet-wielding monk, could keep silent no longer. He got much more than a debate, however. He and his list of Ninety-Five Theses triggered a Reformation that would sweep across his native German lands, across Europe, and eventually across the entire world. The world would never be the same. Luther's act gave birth to the Protestant church, now nearly 600 million members strong. Luther's act also brought the world out of medieval times and into the modern age. Little wonder historians like the date of October 31, 1517.

While we like that date, and Luther for that matter, the Reformation is a much broader event than that singular day. To be sure, the Reformation began on that day. The Reformation, however, spanned two centuries and encompassed a cast of characters from a variety of nations. Luther may very well be at the center of the Reformation, but he does not stand alone.

This book offers a look at this cast of characters and what they accomplished for the life of the church. It tells the various stories that make up the one, grand narrative of the Reformation. We move from Germany down to Switzerland, then over to France and back again. We cross the English Channel to see the Reformation in Britain, and we cross the ocean to see the Reformation's impact on the New World. Along the way we meet up with Martin Luther, Ulrich Zwingli, Conrad Grebel, Menno Simons, and John Calvin. We also meet Thomas Cranmer, Kings Henry VIII and Edward VI, John Knox, John Bunyan, Lady Jane Grey,

Anne Bradstreet, and many others. While some of these are rather familiar to us, perhaps we are meeting some of them for the first time.

Before we begin our tour, however, it may be helpful to explore why we should even be talking about these Reformers in the first place. So Chapter One begins with a question of fundamental importance: Why does the Reformation matter to us today?

chapter one

FIVE HUNDRED YEARS OLD AND STILL GOING STRONG

Why the Reformation Matters Today

This book is built upon two ideas. First, the Reformation matters. Second, history can be fun. Since you are reading this book, I'm prone to think that you already believe these two points. It might be worthwhile, however, to spend some time on them before we go any further.

"History is bunk," as Henry Ford so famously put it. Newer is better, it has often been said. If conventional and even presidential wisdom is our guide, then the study of history offers little for life in the twenty-first century. On top of that, it's boring—just one relentless repetition of dates after another. But these estimations of history couldn't be further from the truth.

REMEMBER THE EXODUS

History has always been crucial to the people of God. Again and again the Old Testament authors sound the mantra, "Remember." For them, the rallying cry wasn't "Remember the Alamo." It was "Remember the Exodus." Israel was to remember the Exodus, to remember all that God had done for his people in delivering them from bondage in Egypt and in bringing them into the Promised Land. They were to remember the covenant that governed their relationship with each other and with God (see, for example, Exod. 20:2). When something significant occurred in the life of Israel, they erected a monument so they and future generations would remember what great things God had done for them (see, for example, Josh. 4:1-7). The Israelites did best when they remembered. They flailed and faltered when they forgot. Those who don't know history, as another saying goes, are doomed to repeat it.

History matters no less in the pages of the New Testament. When Christ huddled his disciples one last time before his arrest and crucifixion, he assured them of one precious promise—that the Holy Spirit would come and would help them to remember. He would guide them in remembering and in recording those memories so they would give a true and accurate account of all that Christ did in his life and in his work of redemption on the cross. The Holy Spirit would help them remember and write down for the whole world who Christ was as the God-man and what he did as the Redeemer of his people (John 14, 16).

We see this in the example of Luke and his Gospel. When Luke begins his narrative account of the story, he turns from his profession as a physician to that of historian. He writes to Theophilus:

> *Inasmuch as many have undertaken to compile a narrative of the things that have been accomplished among us, just as those who from the beginning were eyewitnesses and ministers of the word have delivered them to us, it seemed good to me also, having followed all things closely for some time past, to write an orderly account for you, most excellent Theophilus, that you may have certainty concerning the things you have been taught (Luke 1:1-4).*

For Luke, history mattered. The church depended on it. History mattered to Paul too. He tells us that all of his preaching, indeed Christianity itself, hangs on one combined historical event: the death, burial, and resurrection of Jesus Christ (1 Cor. 15:12-18). For the Old Testament it was "Remember the Exodus," an event of redemption that prefigured the work of Christ. For the New Testament, it is "Remember Christ and his cross."

What we learn from all of this is that Christianity isn't a religion of abstraction or of speculative philosophies. God revealed himself in a physical place and in real time. There's no virtual revelation. And the apex of his revelation to his creatures is the incarnate one, the God-man, Jesus Christ, who was born in history, lived in a real place in flesh and blood, and died in plain view. He rose again not in some abstract way but in reality. He appeared to the disciples and to the crowds (Luke 24), and he ate fish on the shores of the Sea of Tiberias (John 21).

Luke doesn't stop his narrative with the resurrection of Christ. His sequel, the book of Acts, picks up the story with the tragedies and triumphs of the early church. It was of utmost importance to Luke that the church remember how God worked and how Christianity began with a tiny band of desperate disciples. To say that history matters to Christianity is a classic understatement.

THE CLASSROOM OF CHURCH HISTORY

But that's *biblical* history. Of course it matters. What about *church* history? Why should it matter? Or to put it directly, we have biblical history, but we don't need church history. Or to put it even more directly, we have the Bible—we don't need *tradition* too.

While it is true that we must be careful never to confuse biblical history and church history, it is not true that we don't need church history. Further, while it is true that we must always preserve the sole authority of Scripture—which, incidentally, is a Reformation principle—it is not true that tradition serves no purpose. We are not the first Christians trying to make sense of the Bible and trying to proclaim it faithfully and winsomely in the world in which we live. We have guides from the past.

Church history provides us with plenty of examples—good, bad, and even ugly—of Christians from all walks of life and from a variety of contexts who labored to bring their faith to bear upon the world in which they lived. Church history is like one grand classroom focused on living out Christ's final command to his church—to be disciples in the world (John 17:9-21). When we remember the lessons, we tend to do well. When we forget or ignore them, we tend to stumble.

"HERE I RAISE MY EBENEZER"

This line, from the second stanza of Robert Robinson's hymn "Come, Thou Fount of Every Blessing," comes from 1 Samuel 7:10-12. *Ebenezer* means "stone of help." God "helped" Israel by confounding the Philistine army and defeating them. So Israel would always remember what God did for them, Samuel erected a monument, naming it Ebenezer. The hymn uses this text to stress the importance of remembering, of looking over the scenes of our life and seeing God's hand at work. As the full line declares, "Here I raise my Ebenezer; hither by thy help I'm come."

> As Samuel was offering up the burnt offering, the Philistines drew near to attack Israel. But the LORD thundered with a mighty sound that day against the Philistines and threw them into confusion, and they were routed before Israel. And the men of Israel went out from Mizpah and pursued the Philistines and struck them, as far as below Beth-car. Then Samuel took a stone and set it up between Mizpah and Shen and called its name Ebenezer; for he said, "Till now the LORD has helped us." (1 Sam. 7:10-12)

But church history is more than a classroom that keeps us from stumbling. It can also be humbling. "Newer is better" has a certain ring of pride to it. It is as if we are saying we are so much better than those in the past, so much smarter, so much more clever. It is true that technology has advanced and time has marched on. Imagine what Luther would think of our twenty-first-century world. Yet I marvel at what Luther did accomplish. His collected writings in German are over one hundred volumes; the English edition taxes readers at its abridged fifty-six volumes. And he did all that with quill and ink and movable type that took hours on end to arrange. When you look at what Luther accomplished—his books, his sermons, his hymns, his teaching, his founding and building the denomination that bears his name—you might think he lived ten lifetimes. We in our age with everything we have at our disposal should be humbled by these accomplishments.

We are also humbled by the depth of the Reformers' devotion to Christ. We talk much about the spiritual disciplines in our contemporary times, but the Puritans wrote the book on the matter. J. I. Packer likens the Puritans to the great California Redwoods, towering in their spiritual maturity and insight. In some ways we are not standing on their shoulders—we are standing in their shadows. Studying the various figures in church history, and especially the lives of the Reformers, can be a humbling experience, an experience that we, basking in the hubris of the twenty-first century, sometimes desperately need.

Finally, we are not only taught humility, we are also taught about what matters most when we look to church history and the Reformation in particular. The Reformation was a time of great challenge for those who longed to be true to the Word of God. They debated and wrote. They preached and prayed and were imprisoned. Some gave their very lives for what they believed. This was a crisis moment. In times of crisis, the peripheral and non-essential has a way of dropping off, leaving one with what is central and essential, with those things that matter most.

REFORMATION

The word *reformation* comes from the Latin verb *reformo*, which means "to form again, mold anew, or revive." The Reformers did not see themselves as inventers, discoverers, or creators. Instead they saw their efforts as rediscovery. They weren't making something from scratch but were reviving what had become dead. They looked back to the Bible and to the apostolic era, as well as to early church fathers such as Augustine (354–430) for the mold by which they could shape the church and re-form it. The Reformers had a saying, "*Ecclesia reformata, semper reformanda,*" meaning "the church reformed, always reforming."

THE LESSONS OF THE REFORMATION

The things that matter most to us all center on the gospel. The church simply can't afford to forget the lesson of the Reformation about the utter supremacy of the gospel in everything the church does. Elie Wiesel, Nobel Prize winner and Holocaust survivor, has dedicated his life to bearing witness to the unimaginable horrors and atrocities of the Holocaust. He speaks of the unspeakable. And he does so because humanity cannot afford to forget the lesson of the Holocaust. It is far too easy to forget, especially when forgetting eases our conscience. History, however, compels us to remember. In studying the Reformation, we remember what the church is all about, and we remember how easy it is for the church to lose its grip on the gospel.

If he said it once, Martin Luther said it a hundred times: "The church's true treasure is the gospel." Luther lived at a time when this true treasure had been traded for something worth far less. As a monk, he stood in a long line of succession that stretched back through centuries of theologians and churchmen who had heaped up layer upon layer of extrabiblical teaching and practice, obscuring the church's true treasure of the gospel. Like scaffolding that surrounds and hides the beauty of a building, these layers needed to be torn down so the object that mattered could be seen without hindrance and without obstruction. Luther, with a little help from his friends, tore down the scaffolding, revealing the beauty and wonder of the gospel for the church once again. Luther called his own (re)discovery of the gospel a "breakthrough" (*durchbruch* in German).

In the process he brought about an entire revolution of church life, practice, and doctrine. Many of the doctrines that we Protestants take for granted find their crystallized expression in the thought of the Reformers. Theologians speak of the *Solas*, from the Latin word *sola*, meaning "alone." Usually we list five *Solas*:

• 1. *Sola Scriptura*, meaning "Scripture alone": The Bible is the sole and final authority in all matters of life and godliness. The church looks to the Bible as its ultimate authority.

• 2. and 3. *Sola Gratia*, meaning "grace alone," and *Sola Fide*, meaning "faith alone": Salvation is by grace alone through faith alone. It is not by works; we come to Christ empty-handed. This is the great doctrine of justification by faith alone, the cornerstone of the Reformation.

• 4. *Solus Christus*, meaning "Christ alone": There is no other mediator between God and sinful humanity than Christ. He alone, based on his work on the cross, grants access to the Father.

• 5. *Soli Deo Gloria*, meaning "the glory of God alone": All of life can be lived for the glory of God; everything we do can and should be done for his glory. The Reformers called this the doctrine of *vocation*, viewing our work and all the roles we play in life as a calling.

These doctrines form the bedrock of all that we believe, and the Reformers gave these doctrines their finest expression. In addition to the doctrines we routinely believe, the Reformers also laid out for us many of the practices of the church that we take for granted. The church had lost sight of the sermon, celebrating the Mass instead. The Reformers returned the sermon to the church service. In the case of the Puritans in England, they returned it with a vengeance.

Congregations didn't sing in the centuries leading up to the Reformation. In fact, Jan Hus, one of the pre-Reformation reformers, was condemned as a heretic for, among other things, having his congregation sing. Luther and the other Reformers restored congregational singing to the church. Knowing this should humble us every time we sing in church. We should offer our heartfelt thanks to Luther, and we should remember what Hus gave for the privilege.

JAN HUS (1372–1415)

Priest and rector of Bethlehem Chapel in Prague, Czech Republic (then Bohemia), Hus was a forerunner of the Reformation. Inspired by the ideas of John Wycliffe, Hus held to the authority of Scripture, a view that led him to challenge many practices of the Roman Catholic Church. He wrote against papal authority and, as Luther would later do in the Ninety-Five Theses, against indulgences. He proposed a Bible translation into Czech, congregational singing, and the preaching of the Bible. For these views he was condemned and martyred. A century later Martin Luther would take his stand for these same ideas.

Jan Hus

The Reformers also revolutionized daily life outside the church. They gave new meaning to work and to various roles—spouses, parents, and children; employees and employers; civic rulers and citizens. Prior to the

Reformation, the only work that really mattered was church work. The rest of life was simply viewed as putting in time.

In the chapters that follow, we'll have much more to say on these doctrines, church practices, and views on life and work. The Reformers have left us a significant legacy on all these matters. Sometimes these are lessons that we still need to learn.

DO WE STILL NEED THE REFORMATION?

So far we have been assuming that the Reformation matters because it serves the church and because it was a most valuable time in the church's life when so many had lost their way. Some, however, have a different opinion of the Reformation's value.

The dean of American church historians, Mark Noll, has recently published a book with a rather provocative title, *Is The Reformation Over?*[1] Noll and coauthor Carolyn Nystrom offer an answer that will be hotly debated. They say, yes, the Reformation is over. This book represents one particular viewpoint that stretches back to another hotly debated document entitled "Evangelicals and Catholics Together" (ECT). This document speaks of the newfound unity between Roman Catholics and Evangelicals "nearly five hundred years after the divisions of the Reformation era."[2]

This approach views the Reformation as a necessary and most helpful corrective of a medieval Roman Catholic church gone quite bad and adrift from the gospel and the authority of Scripture. But times have changed, some argue. Consequently, the Reformation is over. Instead of trumping the Catholic/Protestant distinction, we should seek unity within the church, a unity that attempts to bridge the Protestant/Roman Catholic divide.

In other circles, such as recent movements within the Anglican Church, the Reformation is seen much more negatively. It is seen as the source of division and strife, an unfortunate occurrence in the life of the church, and a sin of the past that must be atoned for. This views the Reformation not as a breakthrough but as a breakdown of the unity of the church, a failure to live up to Christ's command that the church be one (John 17:23).[3]

Luther and the other Reformers cast their vote for unity, but not for unity at all costs. The ecumenical spirit of our contemporary age neglects the caution of the Reformers, establishing a Christian unity that is built on the flimsiest theological foundations. Against the current drive for ecumenicism and even for pluralism, the Reformers remind us that unity apart from a solid biblical and theological base builds a grand castle on mere sand.

There are also those within Evangelicalism or Protestantism who look askance at the Reformation. They see the Reformation as causing too many divisions, too many denominations. They don't seek unity across the Roman Catholic/Protestant divide, but they do seek unity within Protestantism. They see the Reformers as classic theological nitpickers, too concerned over minutiae, who unnecessarily split the church. They cringe to think of all the denominations left to us by the Reformation and cry out for unity.

Against all of these challenges to the Reformation, we need to realize that the Reformers saw nothing less than the gospel at stake. We sometimes forget what Luther, Calvin, Zwingli, and others risked in taking a stand for the gospel. They risked their very lives. Regarding the Reformers' work as nothing more than sowing seeds of unfortunate division shows both little knowledge of and little respect for what they did. They were human, and they had their faults and shortcomings. They sinned, sometimes greatly. But they also, like the imperfect characters of the Bible, were used greatly by God. In other words, the church should be grateful for the Reformation. And in this age of religious pluralism, theological laxity, and biblical illiteracy, perhaps the Reformation is needed more than ever before.

Prior to the Reformation, there were various attempts to reform the church. Some movements addressed issues of church leadership and government, trying to wrest control from the papacy. Other groups tried to reform the extravagance of the church and its pursuit of wealth. Others addressed the lackluster spirituality that was all too prevalent. These movements could put their finger on the problem—they just couldn't arrive at a solution. All of these movements failed where the Reformation succeeded. The reason? The Reformation got to the heart of the matter:

right theology. The Reformers rightly diagnosed the disease, and they rightly administered the necessary cure.

Today we can fall into the same trap as those failed movements that attempted reform. We can put our trust in programs. We can rely on new leadership or the application of innovative management techniques. We can count on moral reform. The Reformation sounds a clarion call of caution to all such attempts. If we as a church don't get it right on the doctrines of the Bible, Christ, and salvation, we'll never head in the right direction, no matter how innovative or energetic or zealous we may be.

THE HUMAN SIDE OF HISTORY

I mentioned that this book is built on two foundational beliefs. We have been discussing the first one, the belief that the Reformation matters. Here is the second: *history can be fun.* I'm almost convinced, with apologies to my colleagues, that history teachers themselves are responsible for history's bad reputation. We have sometimes been so concerned with the vital task of conveying information that we have neglected to see the people we teach about as flesh and blood, as three-dimensional characters. In the quest to convey dates and facts, we have failed to see the people of history in their family roles and dealing with the foibles of life. We have often missed their sense of humor, their sense of wonder at life.

History is only boring if we make it so. In the chapters to follow, I have endeavored to show these Reformers, these towering Redwoods as J. I. Packer calls them, as real people who lived with both feet on earth. I have tried to tell their very human stories.

I once read a review of a biography by the niece of the subject. She thought the biography superb in every way except one. The author failed, she thought, to display her uncle's sense of humor. She commended the author's careful discussion of his life and his insightful take on the complex issues of his thought. But she was always struck by her uncle's sense of humor. And on that count she thought the biography fell short of telling the true and full story of her uncle's life. We must always think of our larger-than-life heroes from church history as human beings. We need to see them laughing. As that niece reminds us, until we see them laughing, we really haven't seen them at all.

Of course, life isn't always laughter. Just as we experience in our own lives, these figures faced trials and tragedies. Martin Luther, by all accounts, knew how to laugh. He also knew how to cry. We not only see the Reformers laughing at their own foibles and at the ironies of life—we also see them struck by the trials of illness and betrayal, by the sheer frustration of life's limitations. We learn from their writings and work. We also learn from the example of their extraordinary and everyday lives.

CONCLUSION

We study the Reformation because of what we can learn. We learn of the treasure of the gospel. We learn how easy it can be for the church to lose sight of its value. We learn of the origin of most of the practices of church life that we simply take for granted. We learn what doctrines should matter most. We learn how to proclaim those doctrines in the world in which we live. And we learn about real people, gifted and talented, who also possessed the flaws and limitations of humanity. Above all, we learn from them that our faith and trust lie not ultimately in their lives and in their examples, but in the God-man, Jesus Christ. They all point us beyond themselves to him. Luther said it best: "We are beggars."

chapter two

A MONK AND A MALLET

Martin Luther and the German Reformation

It's very hard for a man to believe that God is gracious to him.
The human heart can't grasp this.

MARTIN LUTHER

Martin Luther died within eyeshot of the font where he was baptized as an infant. During his remarkable lifetime he had seen the entire western world change. Born on November 10, 1483, Luther entered a world dominated by the Roman Catholic Church. By the time of his death on February 18, 1546, that institution was crumbling. And that was due in no small part to the lawyer turned monk turned reformer.[1]

Luther had pried open the lock that the Roman Catholic Church had on worship, on the sacraments, on religious life, and above all on the gospel. He pointed the church back to its sure foundation of God's Word and the gospel, laying the foundation for the Protestant Reformation that would encompass Ulrich Zwingli's efforts in Zurich, John Calvin's in Geneva, and John Knox's in Scotland. All by swinging a mallet.

THE SHOULDERS LUTHER STOOD ON

Luther wasn't the first to challenge the Roman Catholic Church; he had many shoulders upon which to stand. These include Peter Waldo (c. 1170) in France. Waldo used his own resources to launch a reform movement, overseeing a translation of the Latin Vulgate into French and establishing a dedicated group of itinerant preachers of the gospel. His followers, known as Waldenses, exist to this day. In England, John Wycliffe (1329–1384), the so-called "Morningstar of the Reformation," led the charge. Three of his many works deserve mention. First is the Wycliffe Bible, an English translation of the Latin Vulgate that was largely done by a team. The other two are *Civil Dominion* (1376), challenging the Holy Roman Empire's ascendancy over Great Britain, and *Divine Dominion* (1375), challenging the supremacy of the Roman Catholic Church and the authority of the pope. Wycliffe died of a stroke. A posthumous trial found him guilty of heresy. His bones were exhumed and burned. In addition to Waldo and Wycliffe, many others risked their lives in speaking out against the abuses of the church. Luther himself acknowledged his debt to their efforts. He stood upon their shoulders.

LUTHER BEFORE HE BECAME A LUTHERAN

Like most significant figures in history, Luther felt he was not suited for the part he was called to play.[2] "Who would have divined," Luther recalled later in life, "that I would receive a Bachelor's and then a Master's of Arts, then lay aside my [law] student's cap and leave it to others in order to become a monk . . . and that despite all I would get in the pope's hair—and he in mine—and take a runaway nun for my wife? Who would have predicted this for me?" His intense religious conscience, putting it mildly, might have been an indicator that he was headed for the monastery. His father, however, had other plans, working and sacrificing so his son would receive the best education of the day and enter the noble profession of law. Luther took to his studies, excelling in his classes and making his way quite well. But his spiritual anxieties (the German word is *anfechtungen*, which means a soul-struggle or a deep anxiety) seemed to dog him at every turn.

An early turning point in Luther's life came as he traveled back to Erfurt, where he had just taken his M.A. in law, after visiting his parents in Mansfield. A violent thunderstorm caught up with Luther. He took it to be the very judgment of God upon his soul. He clung to the only mediator he knew, or at least the only mediator he dared approach—St. Anne, the patron saint of miners, his father's profession. He cried out, "Help me, St. Anne, and I will become a monk." He survived the storm and made good on his vow. His troubles, however, did not find resolution in the monastery. In fact, Luther's struggles intensified.

SEND HIM TO ROME

His wise abbot, Johann Von Staupitz, recognized Luther's potential for the church if only the young monk could get over his struggles. He prescribed a pilgrimage to Rome, thinking that a visit to the Holy See would set things right in Luther's soul. What Luther found at Rome, amidst its hypocrisy and facade and chicanery, however, only served to disillusion him further. Staupitz next sent Luther to study theology. *Luther will be so busy,* Staupitz reasoned, *that he won't have time for his intractable self-examination.* Again the cure proved worse than the disease. As Luther earned another Master's degree, this time in theology, received his doctorate, and began lecturing in theology, he was driven back to the writings of Augustine and from there to Paul. What he found at first seemed an insurmountable obstacle: he was unrighteous, and the holy God demanded righteousness.

Martin Luther

This plagued Luther much more than it did his contemporaries. They had, curiously enough, a rather low view of the righteousness of God, thinking that this standard could be met by merely racking up enough merits, enough righteous deeds. Luther knew it wasn't a matter of quantity but of quality. We are not merely sinners because we sin; we are sinners at the very root of our being. Sin isn't just a matter of what

27

we do; it's a matter of who we are. And nothing we can do, even if we are considered saints, can overcome that. But at this point in Luther's life, in the early- to mid-1510s, he saw no solution to the dilemma. He concluded that, like a tyrant, a righteous God demanded of his unrighteous subjects something they could not give. He no longer feared God; now he hated him.

AN ARTIST AND A CEILING

Luther first tried to draw attention to the ineffective way the church was dealing with the problem of humanity's sinfulness on October 31, 1517. The date is important. It was All Hallow's Eve, the day before All Saints' Day. On that day, pilgrims would file past the relics in the church and would appeal to the excess merits of the saints in hopes of pleasing the righteous demands of God. Of course, this occurred every year, but this year was different. Two things in particular converged. First, Luther's study and teaching had been leading him to conclusions very different from the teachings of the Roman Catholic Church. Second, an artist was busy painting a ceiling.

Now this wasn't just any artist, and this wasn't just any ceiling. It was Michelangelo and the Sistine Chapel of St. Peter's Cathedral in Rome. Leo X's extravagant tastes in art had all but bankrupted the Vatican treasury. Albert of Mainz had already overstepped his bounds in taking two bishoprics at too young an age, and now he wanted a third—and the money and power that went along with them. It was against church law, however; only a papal dispensation could make it happen. Leo X and Albert were both businessmen who knew how to strike a deal. They agreed on a price of 10,000 ducats—presumably sanctifying the deal by considering the figure as standing for the Ten Commandments. Now Albert could have his third bishopric. But one last roadblock remained. Albert, whose wealth consisted more of land than hard currency, didn't have the money he'd pledged. Enter his enterprising and resourceful monk, Johann Tetzel.

Tetzel had devised a scheme involving an indulgence sale. Indulgences were pardons for sin, a practice that started during the Crusades. In order to muster knights to go on crusades, popes would offer indulgences from sin and from purgatory for those who fought. Nobles wanted the benefits but without the potential cost of their lives or the lives of their sons. So they would hire peasants to go in their place. The peasants' families would get money, and the nobles would get the indulgences. In the time between the Crusades and Luther, this practice of indulgences evolved—or rather devolved—into simply buying indulgences for sin directly from the church. "Repentance" could be bought.

Tetzel seized on the indulgence practice to fill Albert's coffers. In fact, Tetzel's campaign, with the pope's blessing, was an unprecedented indulgence sale that would forgive sins past, present, and future. And in his entrepreneurial spirit Tetzel even devised a marketing campaign of sermons—"Can you hear your dead relatives screaming out in pain in purgatory while you fiddle away your money?" he preached—and even an advertising jingle:

When a coin in the coffer rings,
a soul from Purgatory springs.

Tetzel hawked his indulgences, guaranteed by the pope's signature, in Albert's territory. Once word of it got out, however, the faithful from all over Germany thronged to buy one. Among them were Luther's parishioners. Luther could be "silent no more," his own words. He posted his Ninety-Five Theses in the hopes of stirring a debate in which the best minds would grapple with the problem of buying salvation.[3]

Of course, Luther had some jabs in the Ninety-Five Theses as well. Thesis #50 is rather straightforward: "Christians are to be taught that if the pope knew the exactions of the indulgence preachers, he would rather that St. Peter's church should go to ashes than that it should be built up with the skin, flesh, and bones of his sheep." This was followed in the next thesis by a reference to "hawkers of pardons [or indulgences] who cajole money." Luther could also get right to the heart of the matter theologically. "The true treasure of the church," thesis #62 informs us, "is the most holy gospel of the glory and grace of God."[4]

Leo X wasn't interested in a debate, especially a theological one. In fact, at first Leo X simply dismissed Luther. "The ramblings of a drunken

German," he said when he first read the Ninety-Five Theses, adding that Luther will "think differently when he sobers up."

Though the Ninety-Five Theses stop short of articulating the heart of Reformation theology, they do point to the problems plaguing the medieval Roman Catholic Church. It would take more writings and more run-ins with the pope before Luther would arrive at the crystal-clear expression of the gospel and of the doctrine of justification by faith. But when he nailed those Ninety-Five Theses to the church door, you could see the breach in the walls of the dam. The floods soon began.

"I'LL TAKE FIVE *SOLAS* TO GO, PLEASE"

From 1517 until 1521, Luther was constructing the planks of Reformation theology: *Sola Scriptura, Sola Fide, Sola Gratia, Solus Christus*, and *Soli Deo Gloria*.[5] When Luther was caught in that thunderstorm, his thoughts were not turned to Christ. He instead reflexively turned to St. Anne. Luther came to realize, however, the futility of looking to a mediator besides Jesus. This led him to the conviction that humanity's only mediator is Christ (1 Tim. 2:5)—*Solus Christus*, Christ alone.

Theologians often refer to Luther's "theology of the cross." For Luther, everything leads to, emanates from, and centers on the cross of Christ. In the Heidelberg Disputation of 1517 Luther declares, "He deserves to be called a theologian, however, who comprehends the visible and manifest things of God seen through suffering and the cross." We come to God only through Christ, and we come to Christ on the cross, for he bears the penalty of our sin and suffers in our place (Gal. 3:10-14). This insight provided Dietrich Bonhoeffer (1906–1945) with the tools to withstand Hitler and the Nazi regime. It provides all of us with a profound perspective on the supremacy of Christ in his humility and suffering.

LUTHER'S BREAKTHROUGH:
THE REFORMATION (RE)DISCOVERY

In his preface to the *Complete Edition* of his Latin Writings (1545) Luther writes:

> Though I lived as a monk without reproach, I felt that I was a sinner before God with an extremely disturbed conscience. I could not believe that he was

placated by my satisfaction. I did not love, yes, I hated the righteous God who punishes sinners, and secretly, if not blasphemously, certainly murmuring greatly, I was angry with God. . . . Thus I raged with a fierce and troubled conscience. Nevertheless, I beat importunately upon Paul at that place [Rom. 1:17] most ardently desiring to know what St. Paul wanted.

At last, by the mercy of God, meditating day and night, I gave heed to the context of the words, namely, "For in [the gospel] the righteousness of God is revealed from faith for faith, as it is written, 'The righteous shall live by faith.'" There I began to understand that the righteousness of God is that by which the righteous lives by a gift of God, namely by faith. And this is the meaning: the righteousness of God is revealed by the gospel, namely the passive righteousness with which the merciful God justifies us by faith, as it is written, "The righteous shall live by faith." Here I felt that I was altogether born again and had entered paradise itself through open gates. . . . And I extolled my sweetest words with a love as great as the hatred with which I had before hated the words "righteousness of God." Thus that place in Paul was for me the very gate to paradise.

Luther not only changed in his view of other mediators—he also changed in his view of God, the righteous Judge. He expressed this in a grammar lesson. The righteousness that God demands is not active but passive. In other words, it's not a righteousness we earn—it is one earned for us. We are not justified before God by our works or merits, Luther argued, but by faith alone through grace alone—*Sola Fide* and *Sola Gratia*. This is the great doctrine of justification by faith alone. Luther no longer hated God. In fact, he came to love God and to love the words, "the righteousness of God." His fear and anger melted away.

During this time, 1517–1521, the rift between Luther and the pope grew. The pope excommunicated him, calling him a wild boar. Luther returned by calling the pope the Antichrist. The showdown came at the Diet of Worms in the spring of 1521. Expecting a debate, Luther was instead asked two questions. Pointing to the heap of writings before him on the table, Luther's accusers asked him if those were his writings. He said yes. Then he was asked to recant. Luther took a day to think about it.

The next day Luther once again stood before the impressive gathering of church and civil officials and was again asked to recant his writings. Boldly he proclaimed:

Since then your serene majesty and your lordships seek a simple answer, I will give it in this manner, plain and unvarnished: Unless I am convinced by the testimony of the Scriptures or by clear reason, for I do not trust either in the pope or in councils alone, since it is well known that they often err and contradict themselves, I am bound to the Scriptures I have quoted and my conscience is captive to the Word of God. I cannot and I will not retract anything, since it is neither safe nor right to go against conscience. I cannot do otherwise. Here I stand. May God help me, Amen.

Luther's answer expresses the Reformation plank of *Sola Scriptura.* Scripture is the authority for the church. It alone is the very Word of God.

That leaves one final Reformation *sola, Soli Deo Gloria.* Luther stumbled across this through his use of the word *vocation.* In his day, *vocatio,* Latin for "calling," only applied to church work. Monks, nuns, and priests all had a calling, a special task. Others simply worked. Luther applied *vocatio* to all the professions and to all the various roles that we play. Being a husband, son, or father or wife or daughter or mother was a calling. So too was being a farmer or a miner or a stonemason. All of life could and should be lived for the glory of God alone. Luther was inspired by Paul. If we can eat and drink to the glory of God, then everything can be done for the glory of God (1 Cor. 10:31).

The Castle at Wartburg

Later a German musician would subscribe to this teaching of Luther. So Johann Sebastian Bach would sign his pieces, both pieces commissioned for the church and his so-called secular works, JSB and SDG. JSB stands, of course, for his initials; SDG stands for *Soli Deo Gloria*. Luther and Bach, both significant figures from the pages of history, remind us that in our seemingly ordinary work and life we are doing something extraordinary. Francis Schaeffer said it well: "There are no little people, no little places."[6] When we live life, all of it, for the glory of God, we are engaged in the most profound of activities. We are doing something that matters truly and ultimately. In the service of the glory of God there is nothing little at all.

Philip Melanchthon

THE LUTHERAN CHURCH AFTER LUTHER

After Luther's death in 1546, the mantle of leadership fell to Philip Melanchthon (1497–1560). A prodigy, Melanchthon arrived at Wittenberg in 1519 as a twenty-year-old professor who had already written a Greek grammar. He and Luther struck a deep bond, though they were of a different temperament— Luther once said that Melanchthon would use pins and needles to stab when he himself would use a large spear. Melanchthon tended toward a softer edge than his mentor and could be known for compromise. In the wake of Luther's death, a number of controversies stirred the church, including Lutheran/Catholic relations, the doctrines of justification by faith and predestination, and views of the Lord's Supper. Some contend that Melanchthon mishandled these controversies, setting the church on a trajectory that would stray from Luther's teaching. Melanchthon's legacy within the church is a contested one.

The Book of Concord (1580) comprises the official documents of the Lutheran Church. This consists of the Augsburg Confession (1530), various documents written by Luther and Melanchthon, and the Formula of Concord (1577).

LUTHER'S RIB

Luther was a confirmed bachelor. Or so he thought. Luther found his match in an escaped nun, Katharina von Bora. Escaping from a convent, or helping someone else escape, was risky and dangerous, causing people to get quite creative in pulling it off. She made her valiant escape in a rather unseemly manner—in a fish barrel. Luther and his friend Leonard Koppe concocted the plan. Koppe, a fish merchant, made his normal delivery to the convent with a wagon full of fish barrels. Once emptied of their contents of haddock, they were driven out not empty but filled with a dozen nuns. All were led away safely, albeit far from luxuriously. Koppe drove them all the way to Wittenberg, where Luther was supposed to find them husbands.

One proved quite picky, interminably so. Luther, while all for marriage, was not looking to take the plunge himself. For one, he was an outlaw, in fact under a sentence of death, and he didn't want to subject a family to such a burden. For another, he had grown rather attached to his bachelor life. Katie soon convinced him otherwise.

When they married, Luther admittedly didn't do it for love. It was to give his parents grandchildren and to get back at the pope—reasons that certainly wouldn't impress a young maiden. Nevertheless, Katie persisted in her quest and soon won over Luther's heart. Their love grew and blossomed into one of the greatest love stories of church history. Luther called her "Katy, my rib." "There is no sweeter union," he once said, "than that in a good marriage." He couldn't live without her and their sweet union together.[7]

They had six children of their own and adopted six more, orphaned by one of the many plagues that swept through Europe during those times. One of their children died in infancy; another, the apple of her father's eye, passed away at the age of twelve. Grief nearly overwhelmed

Luther on both occasions, God's grace and the bonds of love with his remaining family bringing him back from the brink of utter depression.

The recent movie on Luther stops at 1530 and the event of signing the Augsburg Confession, curiously just like the old black-and-white from 1953.[8] This is understandable, to a certain extent. The time of action spans from 1517 until 1530. But it's important to realize that Luther lived until 1546.

By the end of his life he had much cause for joy and much cause for sorrow. His precious family circle experienced death. He was villainized by former friends. For much of his life he was an outlaw with a death penalty hanging over his head. He suffered physically, his constitution never quite recovering from his ascetic days as a monk. He was given to times of depression. He doubted. And like Jacob, he wrestled with God. Luther's theology wasn't formed in a vacuum. He did not have the pleasure of a cool, undetached ivory tower to develop his thought. He formed his theology in the trenches, in the trials of life. And he formed it in life's ordinary, everyday experiences. His was a theology full of and fully engaged in life. In fact, for some it was all too full of life.

LUTHER'S EARTHY SIDE

In the middle of a conversation with students around his table about the challenges faced in living the Christian life, Luther once said—and it may shock you, especially if you're prone to blush, "But I resist the devil, and often it is with a fart that I chase him away." On occasion some unseemly language would spill from his lips. He liked to recall a story of a burial of a Roman Catholic priest. As the body lay in the grave, those attending the service set down the holy water, which was to be poured into the grave. A dog happened by and did what dogs do into the bowl. Luther then delivered the punch line: "Even the dogs are becoming Lutheran." For better or for worse, that's Martin Luther. If ever history afforded us a one-of-a-kind, it is he.[9]

I don't mention these incidents because I think Luther was on par with junior high boys in a locker room. I share them because they remind us that Luther was human. He wouldn't measure up against Victorian standards, that much is true. But he never mistook prudishness and

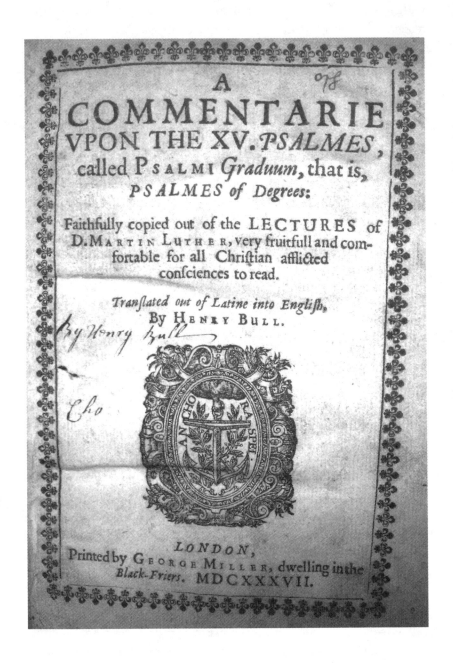

A
COMMENTARIE
VPON THE XV. *PSALMES*,
called PSALMI *Graduum*, that is,
PSALMES of Degrees:

Faithfully copied out of the LECTURES of
D. MARTIN LUTHER, very fruitfull and comfortable for all Christian afflicted
consciences to read.

Translated out of Latine into English,
By HENRY BULL.

LONDON,
Printed by GEORGE MILLER, dwelling in the
Black-Friers. MDCXXXVII.

English Edition of Luther's Psalms Commentary

stuffiness for piety and spirituality. He knew what to take seriously, and he knew never to take himself too seriously. Luther had a body, and it got old, and he liked to poke fun at it.

THE QUOTABLE LUTHER

On Theology
I didn't learn my theology all at once. I had to ponder over it ever more deeply, and my spiritual trials were of help to me in this, for one does not learn anything without practice.

On God
A mighty fortress is our God, a bulwark never failing.

On His Debate with Rome
The time for silence is past, and the time to speak has come.

On Christian Liberty
A Christian is a perfectly free lord of all, subject to none.
A Christian is a perfectly dutiful servant of all, subject to all.

On Raising Children
One must punish in such a way that the rod is accompanied by the apple. It's a bad thing if children and pupils lose their spirit on account of their parents and teachers.

On Preaching
When I have nothing more to say, I stop talking.

Luther didn't care much for pretension. His favorite group to joke about was theologians, which is to say himself. He once chastised Zwingli for speaking in Greek. "God makes fools of both theologians and princes," he said. God does this to remind them that he alone is wise and powerful. Otherwise "we would become presumptuous and would claim wisdom and power for ourselves." Luther knew all too well that he was human, "a stupid clod," as he liked to say.[10]

This view of human nature's foibles and frailty only fueled Luther's vision of God and his goodness. Stripped of humanity's pretensions and pride, he could say, "Our Lord God has made the best gifts most common. The preeminent gift given to all living things is the eye. Small birds have very bright eyes, like little stars, and can see a fly a room-length away. But we don't acknowledge such everyday gifts. We are stupid clods." On another occasion, overwhelmed by the wonder of life's mysteries, Luther exclaimed as he sat playing with one of his children, "Oh, this is the best of God's blessings."[11]

There is so much that can and should be said about Luther. But in all that is said, we must see him bouncing a child on his knee and marveling at the goodness of God to his creatures, especially to flawed and sinful human beings. We need to see him laughing with his students and at himself. And we need to see him clinging to the cross.

CONCLUSION

It is fitting that we still remember Martin Luther today, nearly five centuries after he first posted his famous Ninety-Five Theses on the church door. He was truly larger than life; his legacy is known the world over. Yet, it is most fitting that we remember him because he so ably pointed beyond himself to Christ.

Many churches celebrate Luther and his accomplishments on Reformation Day. It is a day about history, a time to remember what happened in the past. It is also about the present. It is about the power of the gospel to break through the noise and static of the world and to point to Christ. That gospel broke through in the life of a monk bent on getting to heaven through his own efforts. It broke through in a time and a place when the church had lost its way. That God used a monk and a mallet to do it amazed no one more than Luther himself.

Luther was many things, but he was never selfish with the grace of God and the glory of the gospel. "What does it amount to," he asked in a soul-searching way, "that we have the gospel in this little corner? Just reckon that there is no gospel in all of Asia and Africa and that the gospel isn't preached in many parts of Europe, in Greece, Italy, Hungary, Spain, France, England, Poland."[12] So we learn our final lesson from him. Not only should we be steadfast for the gospel, we must be unselfish with it as well. We remember Luther best when we proclaim Christ and the gospel to our world of need. And we do so fully clothed in our humanity.

chapter three

SOME MIDDLE-AGED MEN AND
A SAUSAGE SUPPER

Ulrich Zwingli and the Swiss Reformation

The Word of God shall take its course as surely does the Rhine.
ULRICH ZWINGLI

Picture the scene. Christopher Froschauer, printer and citizen of high
repute in Zurich, has invited a group of men for a sausage supper in
his home. The local priest, Ulrich Zwingli, tops the list. It is reported
that Zwingli, though present, refrains from partaking—a sixteenth-century
version of not inhaling. But not so for the others. They eat freely.

On the surface this event does not appear to have the makings of an
historical occasion. But in reality it does. It changes not only Zurich but
all of Switzerland for centuries. How could such a seemingly conventional
dinner—the Swiss do like their wurst—start a theological revolution?

It was March 1522, and it happened to be Lent, the season in which
such things were not done, especially in the presence of a priest. Two
weeks later Zwingli preached a sermon with arguably one of the greatest
titles of all time: "On the Choice and Freedom of Food." After running
through a number of New Testament texts Zwingli concluded, "These
announcements seem to be enough to me to prove that it is proper for a
Christian to eat all foods." The Lenten fast stemmed from human tradition. Zwingli called such traditions spots on the face of Christ, "unseemly
things, and of the foulness of human commands." Instead Christ will
"become again dear to us, if we properly feel the sweetness of his yoke,
and the lightness of his burden."[1]

39

In April the sermon was printed, taking its place as one of the many writings of Zwingli that would come to circle Europe and beyond. Perhaps a group of middle-aged men eating sausage is not as heroic a picture as a monk swinging a mallet, but it was just as effective. When that group ate a sausage meal and when Zwingli preached his sermon, the Reformation began in Switzerland.

SON OF SWITZERLAND

Born in the shadow of the Alps, Ulrich (or Huldyrich) Zwingli entered the home of Ulrich (Sr.) and Margaretha Zwingli on January 1, 1484—less than two months after the birth of his German counterpart Martin Luther. His father was a shepherd and a magistrate at Wildhaus in the Toggenburg Valley of the Swiss canton of St. Gaul, which is to say that young Zwingli hailed from peasant farmer stock active in politics. Biographers say that as a boy, tending sheep with his father on the steep slopes of the Alps, Zwingli developed one of his guiding principles: patriotism and an unbounded love for his country. Zwingli was Swiss through and through, and as we'll see, his nationalism twice ran him aground. The other guiding principle came to light as he embarked on his studies: an inquisitive and even ravenous mind. Zwingli sought the truth, not resting until he would ferret it out.[2]

HVLRICVS Z VINGLIVS.
Dicitur Hulricus se deuouisse duobus.
Nempe Deo in primis, deinde etiam patriæ
Quam bene persoluit simul is'tis vota duobus,
Pro patria examinis, pro pietate cadis!

Ulrich Zwingli

40

Though of the peasant class, his parents prospered enough to send their son to school. He studied at Berne, then for a brief time at Vienna. His Swiss patriotism contributed to a brief tenure in Austria. He finally settled in for his studies at Basel, taking a B.A. in 1504 and an M.A. in 1506. With degrees and ordination in hand, Zwingli became the priest at Glarus, his boyhood church. He held the post for ten years (1506–1516), his duties interrupted while serving as a chaplain from time to time for Swiss regiments.

THE SWISS CONFEDERATION

In order to have peace in the region and to accommodate free trade, various cities in the modern nation of Switzerland banded together in a loose confederation. Zurich was one of the three founding cantons or regions with a capital city, established in the early 1300s. Each of these cantons maintained their autonomy and sovereignty, Zurich being ruled by a mayor and a twenty-four-member city council, but would band together when necessary. They enjoyed freedom from the Holy Roman Empire and were declared a *reichfrie* or free state. The leaders of the cantons also ruled with a free hand, creating a context that both fostered and appreciated Zwingli's reforms and his sermon "On the Choice and Freedom of Foods."

Known for their soldiering, mercenaries were one of the leading providers of income for the Swiss cantons. Italian and French forces would often hire Swiss mercenaries, and the pope had a standing guard of them, often resulting in Swiss deaths on foreign soils for foreign rulers. At times opposing forces would both have Swiss mercenaries among their ranks, resulting in Swiss killing Swiss, friend and neighbor killing friend and neighbor.

The Battle of Marignano (1515) in the wars between the Valois and the Habsburgs in Northern Italy took nearly ten thousand Swiss lives. And Zwingli served as a chaplain, roaming from body to body administering last rites. He composed a poem during that time and returned to the pulpit at Glarus. Because of his patriotism and nationalism, he began preaching against the mercenary practice. Zwingli had seen enough. But his congregation would not be moved by his appeal, interpreting his anti-mercenary sermons as unpatriotic. They ousted him in 1516.

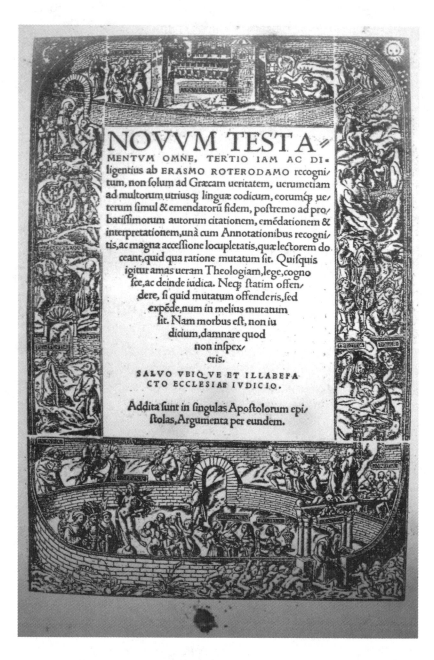

NOVVM TESTA
MENTVM OMNE, TERTIO IAM AC DI
ligentius ab ERASMO ROTERODAMO recogni
tum, non solum ad Græcam ueritatem, ucrumetiam
ad multorum utriusq; linguæ codicum, eorumq; ue
terum simul & emendatoru fidem, postremo ad pro
batissimorum autorum citationem, emédationem &
interpretationem, uná cum Annotationibus recogni
tis, ac magna accessione locupletatis, quæ lectorem do
ceant, quid qua ratione mutatum sit. Quisquis
igitur amas ueram Theologiam, lege, cogno
sce, ac deinde iudica. Necʒ statim offen
dere, si quid mutatum offenderis, sed
expéde, num in melius mutatum
sit. Nam morbus est, non iu
dicium, damnare quod
non inspex
eris.

SALVO VBIQVE ET ILLABEFA
CTO ECCLESIAE IVDICIO.

Addita sunt in singulas Apostolorum epi
stolas, Argumenta per eundem.

Erasmus's Greek New Testament, 1516

42

Zwingli didn't have to travel far to find a new pulpit. Just a few miles down the road was Einsielden, the home of a famous shrine attracting pilgrims, continuing to do so even to the present day. As the people's priest, Zwingli preached to the constant flood of pilgrims. When he wasn't preaching, he was reading and reading and reading. Zwingli was an intellectual first. He often returned to his alma mater, Basel, to keep up with the latest in scholarship. While there, he spent most of his time in conversation with Desiderius Erasmus, who had taken up residence as a visiting scholar in 1514. Zwingli called Erasmus "the most learned of all scholars." Erasmus was there to work on a book, and not just any book, for in two years the printing press in Basel would turn out a text more than one thousand pages in length, *Novum Testamentum Omne*—a complete text of the New Testament in Latin and in Greek.[3]

Desiderius Erasmus of Rotterdam *is* the Renaissance, though he worked with words instead of canvases and marble. Rich in both intellect and personal resources, Erasmus found himself in the vocation of teaching Greek and Hebrew at Oxford. Rarely, however, did students ever take his classes. This freed him to travel widely across the face of Europe pursuing his avocation, the collecting and organizing of Greek manuscripts of the New Testament, and that explains how he ended up at Basel in 1514.

Erasmus of Rotterdam

Everyone—everyone who could read, that is—from priests to scholars, relied on the Latin Vulgate. This Latin text of the Bible was *the* text for the church, partly due to tradition and partly due to necessity. There was no complete Greek text, the original language of the New Testament, nor had there been for centuries. Instead there were Greek manuscripts, literally thousands of manuscripts, in monasteries all over Europe and the Mediterranean regions—the legacy of the tireless labors of monks performing their scribal duties. Erasmus had a remarkable gift for sniffing these manuscripts out. Of course, his personal wealth didn't hamper the efforts in collecting them either. He collated them, publishing in 1516 the *Novum Testamentum Omne*, a critical Greek text of the New Testament alongside the Latin text. For the first time in centuries scholars did not have to rely on a translation of God's Word. They could examine it in its original language.

The Renaissance was known for this kind of thing. *Ad Fontes*, Latin for "To the Fount or Source," became the battle cry. The Renaissance signaled a return to the fount of western culture—the Greeks and Romans with their literature and laws, architecture and art. In the case of the Reformation, *Ad Fontes* means getting beyond what tradition has to say about the Bible and going right to the Bible itself. If there had been no Erasmus with his Greek text, it would have been hard for there to have been a Luther with his *Sola Scriptura* (Scripture alone).

And it would be hard to imagine the Reformation occurring in Switzerland when it did and as it did. A long-awaited copy of Erasmus's text made its way into the hands of Ulrich Zwingli. In fact, one can imagine the conversations Zwingli and Erasmus had from 1514 to 1516, during the two-year process of getting the text published. When Zwingli finally did receive his copy, he devoured it in the second-floor study of his home at Einsielden. He copied out Paul's epistles in Greek and filled the margins with commentary on the text from the church fathers. The next two years, from 1516 to 1518, would be decisive.

These were the years when Luther made his move in Germany, posting his Ninety-Five Theses and engaging in debates with Rome. Zwingli's public moments would come later. For the moment they were private as he turned the pages of the New Testament and rethought all that was around him. Zwingli's friend and his first biographer, Oswald Myconius (1532), has Zwingli wearing his Roman Catholicism uncomfortably all along, telling us Zwingli felt "like a spy in the enemy's camp." Whether or not that's true we don't know. We do know that the seeds of Zwingli's discomfort with Rome were planted early during his studies at Basel in the first years of the sixteenth century. One of his teachers, Thomas Wyttenbach, called indulgences a "cheat and a delusion." Sometime in 1516–1518, Zwingli discovered the real thing, the gospel. Like a snowball rolling downhill, this discovery led to more and more and more. Stripped of all the layers of tradition, Zwingli at last could look into the pages of the Bible and see the glorious gospel of grace. He took that gospel into the pulpit, displaying it for a congregation of sinners in need. The word got around.

In 1518 Zwingli heard of an opening for the position of People's Priest, or preaching pastor, at the Grossmnster, or Great Cathedral, in Zurich. The twin steeples of the church towered over the city, and its history dated back to its founding by Charlemagne in 1090. Zwingli applied, and on his birthday, Saturday, January 1, 1519, he was inducted. He warned the town and church officials that he planned on doing something revolutionary: he was going to preach through the entire New Testament, from *alpha* to *omega*, said the scholar-pastor. The next day as he stood in the pulpit at Zurich he opened his Greek text to Matthew 1:1, reciting the words, "The book of the genealogy of Jesus Christ, the son of David, the son of Abraham." He kept going from there. It took him six years to preach through the New Testament. The city of Zurich would never be the same.

WHAT THE BIBLE HAS TO SAY
ABOUT SAUSAGE

Reading the Bible can be tremendously liberating. Those who were captive to the teaching of the Pharisees and Sadducees in Jesus' day found comfort and solace in words that had long been obscured by tradition and covered over by layer upon layer of human regulations. Paul, quoting the Old Testament, said the righteous shall live by faith in Romans 1:17 and Galatians 3:11. For Zwingli and his congregation, centuries of the church's tradition had transformed the light burden of Christ's grace into a labyrinth of rules and regulations. The righteous were not called to live by faith but by works heaped upon works.

Roman Catholic tradition included feasts and festal seasons with guidelines and procedures. There were vestments to be worn and liturgies and practices to be performed. All of it demanded perfect compliance. Despite natural appetites for bratwurst and sausage, these could not be eaten during Lent. Zwingli, as we have seen, had a problem with that. As he scoured the Scriptures, he looked in vain for any such regulation. The New Testament, he came to find out, did not have much to say about sausage at all.

Not only did he find no prohibition against sausage, he also found no scriptural warrant for a celibate priesthood. In 1522 he along with eleven others wrote and affixed their signatures to a petition with yet another great title: "Petition to Allow Priests to Marry, Or at Least to Wink at Their Marriage." The Roman Catholic authorities wouldn't consent or wink. In a short time Zwingli secretly married Anna Reinhart, a widow. They would eventually have four children, meaning that his secret marriage would eventually become public.[4]

Curiously enough, Zwingli remained friends with the church's powers that be, even receiving a friendly letter from the pope in early 1523. Soon that relationship would come to an end. In 1523 Zwingli led the first of two public debates, known to history as the First and Second Disputation, against Roman Catholic officials before the town council and the citizens of Zurich. For the First Disputation, Zwingli drafted Sixty-Seven Articles. He had two things going for him—his sharp wit and Scripture. He handily won, and the city of Zurich officially broke with the Catholic Church and became Reformed. Other Swiss cities, Basel and Berne among them, would follow. But not all of them would. By 1529 the Swiss Confederation was in a civil war. Once again Zwingli would watch as Swiss fought Swiss, this time for religion and not for money.

UNDERSTANDING GOD'S WORD

While the Reformation was about politics, it wasn't all about politics. It was first and foremost about theology. An invitation came to Zwingli to speak at the Oetenbach Convent. Zwingli accepted, perhaps thinking he might find a wife. After all, Luther married a former nun. Maybe this would be yet another way that Zwingli's career and life would follow Luther's template. So, what would impress these now eligible nuns? A lecture on hermeneutics, of course. Zwingli miscalculated. He returned to Zurich a bachelor, but only for a bit, until he met Anna Reinhart.

The trip to Oetenbach was not a total wash, however, for out of it we have his lecture entitled "Of the Clarity and Certainty of the Word of God," one of the finest pieces of Reformation literature. In this piece Zwingli outlines three major attributes of Scripture, noting that it is powerful, certain, and clear. The Reformation succeeded because it was based on the Word of God. The Bible alone has the *power* to change lives; political pressure and religious formalism both fall miserably short. The Bible can "crush and destroy you" and at the same time lift you up and comfort you; it can "give you joy rather than sorrow." The Bible is also *certain*. From the very beginning in Genesis 1, God says it, and it is. God's word, Zwingli told the Oetenbach nuns, "must always be fulfilled."

ZWINGLI'S SCHOOL OF PROPHECY

Zwingli established an academy in Zurich in 1523 and was named its director (*Schulherr*) in 1525. The main course of study was the Bible in its original languages. Zwingli called the courses the *Prophezei*, meaning "prophets." A Hebrew scholar would read a chapter of the Old Testament in Hebrew and interpret it. Zwingli would follow next, using the Greek translation of the Old Testament (the Septuagint) and selections from the church fathers, giving a "theological exegesis" or interpretation of the text. When Zwingli wasn't reciting Greek, he would teach in Latin. Finally one of the town pastors would comment on how to preach the text or would simply preach a sermon on the text in German. Following Zwingli's death, Heinrich Bullinger assumed the role of director, developing the academy into a modern-day seminary.

As for the Bible's *clarity*, Zwingli tells us, "You must be *theodidacti*, that is, taught by God." We have God's Word, and we have the Holy Spirit, the giver of God's Word. The net result of all of this is, according to Zwingli, that "there is no word that can give greater joy or comfort than his word." It is the very words of eternal life. Zwingli closed his talk with a brief prayer: "May God increase his word in us more and more, and never suffer [allow] us to fall from it. Amen."[5]

It was faithfulness to the Word of God that made the difference between, in the words of one of Zwingli's book titles, *The True and False Religion* (1525). Zwingli saw Roman Catholicism as false, built upon superstition and human tradition. True religion derived from the Bible alone. Consequently Zwingli repudiated the Mass, reduced the number of sacraments from seven to two, rejected the doctrine of purgatory, and dismissed the papal office. Zwingli did think the Bible had something to say about the pope. Like Luther, he called the pope the Antichrist.

FOES TO THE RIGHT AND TO THE LEFT

While he countered Roman Catholicism, Zwingli also faced other theological foes. First, he had his own self and his own overzealous disciples to contend with. Zwingli was committed, perhaps even more than Luther, to the *Sola Scriptura* principle. Simplicity and clarity were to be the signs of the church. If something wasn't in Scripture, it didn't belong in the church. Later Calvin and the Reformed church would develop this principle further as the so-called Regulative Principle: unless a given practice is explicitly mentioned in Scripture, you can't do it in the church.

Zwingli found no scriptural warrant for icons, which flooded the churches in those days. Bands of Reformed priests and craftsmen would enter churches, remove statues and icons, whitewash murals and paintings on church walls, and even remove or cover stained-glass windows. One thing that Zwingli did left him rather internally conflicted. He was a gifted musician. Early in his life some monks even tried to convince his parents to let him pursue a career in music. But he did not find organs in the pages of the Bible. He ordered the pipe organ at the Great Cathedral in Zurich to be locked. By the late 1520s Zwingli pulled back his hand, settling on less extreme measures. But as Lady Macbeth famously says, "What's done cannot be undone." At Zurich such activities were carried out mildly. Other cities, however, tended toward the extreme. Dismembered statues were thrown through the stained-glass windows, and pipe organs were ripped apart.

Zurich

ZWINGLI'S LEGACY

In his decade of reforming Zurich, Zwingli left a lasting legacy. He was followed both at Grossmunster and at the academy in Zurich by Heinrich Bullinger (1504–1575). Bullinger first came into contact with the Reformation while a student at Cologne. The faculty held a book burning of Luther's works, a tacit show of papal allegiance. That only made Bullinger want to read Luther, and when he did, he converted. Bullinger led in bringing the Reformation to Kappel, being an ally of Zwingli's from 1523 on. Bullinger carried on Zwingli's theological and political reforms at Zurich. He crystallized the teaching of Zwingli and the Reformed church in 1566, taking the lead role in The Second Helvetic Confession.

Zwingli, Bullinger, and John Calvin may well be considered the three primary founders of the Reformed movement in Switzerland, which has spawned various denominations. Unlike Luther, Zwingli's name was not given to any denomination. The term Zwinglian or Zwinglianism, however, was coined to identify those who hold to his view of the Lord's Supper as a memorial.

Zwingli not only faced problems with overzealous followers—he also encountered challenges with the Anabaptists. Early on in his reforms, Zwingli was joined by another Catholic priest at Zurich, Conrad Grebel. By 1524 Grebel and others, following Zwingli's lead of scriptural simplicity, would break ranks with him on two matters. First, they saw no basis

49

for infant baptism, holding to believer's baptism only. They even rebaptized themselves, which led to their being called Anabaptists, a term of derision. (*Ana* is a transliteration of the Greek word meaning "again.") Second, they called for a break between church and state, whereas Zwingli held to the connection of the two. In fact, Zwingli proposed that the town council take part in the spiritual discipline of the citizenry. The Anabaptists could not concur.

The Anabaptists were gaining supporters, and Zurich could little afford to be internally divided in the face of Roman Catholic opposition. The City Council exiled Grebel and others. Felix Manz (sometimes spelled Mantz) at first left but then returned. The City Council ordered him to be executed in a most mocking way—by drowning. We will return to the story of the Anabaptists and their beliefs and martyrdoms in Chapter Four. While they shared many beliefs with the Reformed churches in Switzerland, the two groups could not coexist and form a united front.

Neither could the Reformed Church of the Swiss cantons concur with the Lutheran Church in Germany. Phillip of Hesse called a meeting at his castle in Marburg in an attempt to bring these two factions together. They needed each other politically and militarily to withstand the armies of the papal lands. There would be no political alliance, however, without there first being a theological one. Many theologians attended, but the two in the spotlight were Zwingli and Luther. Many theological issues were batted around, but the one that mattered was the Lord's Supper.

Luther rejected the Roman Catholic view of transubstantiation, the belief that the elements of bread and wine become the literal body and blood of Christ.[6] But Luther argued for what he called the *real presence* of Christ, that Christ was above, beneath, and all around the elements. Zwingli took a different approach, interpreting "This is my body" as meaning, "This *signifies* my body." Zwingli's view has come to be termed the memorial view, that the elements are a memorial to Christ and his work on the cross. No theological alliance would be reached, and neither would a political one.[7]

Decades of religious wars ensued as the new Protestant denominations arose from the once dominant Roman Catholic Church and as the various European nation-states arose from the once dominant Holy

Roman Empire. Zwingli himself would become a statistic of the religious wars, dying on the battlefield. Painful births and painful growing processes would fill the sixteenth century as Europe left the medieval era and entered the modern age.

ZWINGLI AND THE PLAGUE

The plague racked Zurich in 1519, taking a third of the lives in that city and nearly taking Zwingli's life as well. After his recovery, the experience gave a sense of urgency to his reforming efforts. He wrote a poem on his experience, entitling the middle stanza "In the Midst of Illness." Apparently it wasn't time for Zwingli to depart this life. He would live for another decade.

"In the Midst of Illness"
Console me, Lord God, console me!
The illness increases, pain and fear seize my body.
Come to me then, with Thy grace, O my only consolation!
It will surely save everyone, who his heart's desire and hopes sets on Thee,
    and who besides despises all gain and loss.
Now all is up. My tongue is dumb, it cannot speak a word.
    My senses are all blighted.
Therefore it is time that Thou conducts my fight hereafter;
Since I am not strong, that I can bravely make resistance to the Devil's wiles
    and treacherous hand.
Still will my spirit constantly abide by Thee, however he rages.

CONCLUSION: OR, WHY WAS ZWINGLI ON THE BATTLEFIELD?

A statue of Zwingli, prominently displayed at the Water Church on the Limmat, has Zwingli standing with a Bible clutched in one hand, a rather large sword in the other. Not quite accurate, for he died with a Bible in one hand and a flag in the other. Nevertheless, the statue represents what may be one of the most troubling things for contemporary onlookers of the Reformers. How could they be blind to the troubles of mixing Scripture and the sword? It is hard for us, especially in our modern context of the separation of church and state, to be sympathetic to this mixture. How could the city council drown Felix Manz? How could

Zwingli, a pastor, take to the battlefield? How could gospel acceptance come about by political coercion?

We should first realize that this was not the era of the separation of church and state. In fact, it was far, far from it. In those days the two had everything to do with each other. The Reformation disrupted the established order of the Holy Roman Empire (historians tell us that in reality it was crumbling anyway), and the fallout took its toll. We in our age have grown accustomed to the notion of a secular state, a state in which politics and even much of daily life transpires outside of and apart from religion and the church. In sixteenth-century Europe there was no such thing as a secular state. This binding of politics and religion resulted in religious wars.

In 1555 at the Peace of Augsburg, the various factions decided on the principle they termed *Cuis regio, Eius Religio*, meaning literally "whose region, their religion." The religion of the leader of any given region was to be the legal religion of that region, whether it was Lutheran, Reformed, or Roman Catholic. Like most political measures, sometimes this accomplished what it was supposed to in keeping the peace, and sometimes it only complicated matters and led to more bloodshed.

None of this is offered as an excuse. Zwingli and the other Reformers have their own consciences to answer to. It is intended, however, to make us sympathetic to their context. They were, after all, children of the age in which they lived. Perhaps we should shy away from a presumptive posture of judgment over them, being humble enough for some self-examination. The Reformers had their blind spots as surely as do we.

We, too, in other words, are children of our age. Later generations of Christians will most assuredly look at us and scratch their heads at what we took for granted to be the right and only way to live out our Christian commitment. Being sympathetic to the Reformers in their political contexts is probably one of the most difficult things for contemporary onlookers to do. Taking time for some healthy self-examination of our own weaknesses is tougher still.

Zwingli's Reformation lasted less than a decade, from attending a sausage supper in 1522 to his death as a chaplain at the Second Battle of Kappel on October 11, 1531. Within these few years Zwingli accomplished more than most do in a lifetime. Studying the Greek New Testament, he stumbled upon the gospel. He committed his life to preaching it to others. In Zurich he reformed church practice, established a school that trained a whole generation of ministers, and led the way for other cities to follow.

In his lifetime Zwingli was painted numerous times. The most famous, by Hans Asper in 1549, perhaps gets him the best. It is a profile, revealing the chiseled features of physical strength from those years on the slopes of the Alps. He is wearing the scholar's cap, always the intellectual. In his hands is the Bible, turned to the pages of Matthew 11, which closes with these words of Christ:

> *Come to me, all who labor and are heavy laden, and I will give you rest. Take my yoke upon you, and learn from me, for I am gentle and lowly in heart, and you will find rest for your souls. For my yoke is easy, and my burden is light.*

chapter four

THE NOT-SO-RADICAL RADICAL REFORMERS

The Anabaptists and the Reformation

Flee the shadow of this world.

MICHAEL SATTLER, MAY 1527,
WHILE IMPRISONED AT BINZDORF

On January 21, 1525, Conrad Grebel baptized George Blaurock. They, along with a few others, were meeting in Blaurock's home in Zurich, and history was about to repeat itself. As we saw in Chapter Three, when a group of theologians get together in a house in Zurich, you can be sure of one thing: something radical is bound to happen. This time it wasn't about sausage. The subject was baptism, and those in the room arrived at the position that baptism is for believers only, not for infants. By the end of the month another eighty or so had joined Blaurock in being baptized. All of them would be named criminals for it.

As early as the fifth century there were laws on the books requiring infant baptism. In the fifteenth century these laws were dusted off and given new life.[1] Grebel, Blaurock, and others such as Felix Manz (alternatively spelled Mantz) were brought before the Zurich town council. They were given a fair debate but were unable to match the honed skills of Ulrich Zwingli—he had, after all, participated in not a few debates. The town council sided with Zwingli. The *ana*-baptizers or re-baptizers (*ana* being the Greek preposition meaning "again") were found guilty and were exiled from Zurich. They were now sojourners and pilgrims, not at home in the Roman Catholic lands and not welcome in Reformed regions. They were disillusioned with the leaders of the Reformation for, in their view, not going far enough to reform the church. They would struggle even well into the next century to find a home. Many of them would lose their lives for their convictions. They were viewed as a threat politically, socially, culturally, and theologically by both Roman Catholicism and the other Reform movements alike. And they were persecuted by both groups.

THEOLOGY ON THE RUN

Writing centuries after the Reformation, B. B. Warfield once remarked about theologians who work in what he called "the cool closets," comfortable surroundings without conflict and challenge. They can hash out their theology with little if any resistance or real-world connections. Then there are those who only know the opposite. They have theologized in the swirl of controversy. No group exemplifies this latter category better than the group led by Michael Sattler (1490–1527) who met at Schleitheim, Switzerland, in 1527. They weren't simply engaged in controversy—they were running for their lives. All of the persecution that Sattler and his fellow Anabaptists faced raised a significant question: *Are these beliefs we hold worth dying for?* Many ended up saying yes. The Anabaptists forged their theology in the crucible.

What's in a Name?

Radical Reformers, Revolutionaries, Anabaptists, Catabaptists—the subjects of this chapter go by many names. In Zurich they were first called *Täufer*, which means Baptists, or *Wiedertaufer*, which means Re-baptists. The leaders of the movement had all been baptized as infants, as Roman Catholics. Their study of Scripture led them to the position that baptism follows a profession of faith, a position that has come to be called believer's baptism or sometimes adult baptism. Consequently they all were baptized again. The preposition *ana* is Greek for "again"; *cata* is another preposition meaning "again."

The name Radical Reformers also needs explaining. Our instinct is to see it as meaning extreme, and indeed some in this broad movement were extreme. But the word *radical* is from the Latin word *radix*, meaning "root." These Radical Reformers differed from the Magisterial Reformers, such as Luther and Zwingli and others. The Radical Reformers thought their counterparts had failed to get at the root of the problem in their reforms of Roman Catholicism—namely, the union of church and state. The Radical Reformers called for a separation of church and state, while the Magisterial Reformers—Zwingli, Luther, and the rest—saw a union, in varying degrees, between church and state. This separation of church and state has become a hallmark of the Radical Reformers even to this present day.

Historian George Huntston Williams has identified three major groups within this movement: the Anabaptists, such as Grebel and Manz; the Spiritualists, such as Kasper Schwenckfeld; and the later Evangelical Rationalists. The Anabaptists or Radical Reformers weren't so troubled about what to call themselves. Most often they just used the title Brethren.

"May joy, peace, and mercy from our Father through the atonement of the blood of Jesus Christ, together with the gifts of the Spirit . . . be to all those who love God." So begins the first theological confession of the Reformation. Affirmed on February 24, 1527, the Anabaptist Schleitheim Confession is not a grand systematic treatise. It is not comprehensive. In fact, it was followed by another Anabaptist confession, the Dordrecht Confession, in 1632 that addresses many crucial areas untouched at Schleitheim. The Schleitheim Confession is not as well known as many of the other Reformation confessions and creedal documents, such as the Westminster Standards. Yet it is a singularly fascinating document in setting forth the distinctives of the Anabaptists.[2]

After its preface, calling for peace in a time of persecution, the Schleitheim Confession enumerates seven articles. The first is a brief statement advocating believer's baptism over infant baptism. Second is a ban for those "who slip and fall into error and sin" after being privately admonished twice. Nowadays this is referred to as shunning. The third article concerns the Lord's Supper, noting that it is for believers only. Fourthly, Schleitheim affirms separation "from the evil and from the wickedness which the devil planted in the world." This includes separation from all things "popish" on the ecclesiastical side and "drinking houses" and "civic affairs" on the civil side.

The fifth article was one of the Anabaptist distinctives that raised Luther's ire. It concerns the clergy, focusing on their moral and character qualifications. It says nothing of being formally trained. In fact, in the early stages the Anabaptists began to downplay formal training, seeing it as a source of pride that exalted human learning. Soon they abandoned formal training of ministers altogether, exhorting ministers to rely on the Holy Spirit instead. Luther and other Reformers couldn't disagree more. To Luther, the future of the church depended on the training of its clergy. He argued that he would not see a medical doctor who merely relied on the Spirit, so why should he entrust himself to untrained physicians of the soul?[3]

The last two articles reveal the distinctive Anabaptist view of church and state. The sixth one, the largest of the articles, asserts pacifism. It acknowledges the "sword" (Rom. 13:4) as ordained of God but quickly adds that the community of Christ must live differently:

> The government magistracy is according to the flesh, but the Christians' is according to the Spirit; their houses and dwelling remain in this world, but the Christians' citizenship is in heaven; the weapons of their conflict and war are carnal and against the flesh only, but the Christians' weapons are spiritual, against the fortification of the evil.

In other words, Christians belong to the kingdom of God and have no part in the workings of the kingdoms of this world.

The seventh article concerns taking oaths, before the Confession concludes with a solemn admonition to keep the community of Christ pure: "Eliminate from you that which is evil and the Lord will be your God and you will be His sons and daughters."

You don't find a great deal of theologizing in the Schleitheim Confession. No detailed discussion of the Trinity, the Bible, or the nature of sin or salvation. Instead you find a community bent on carving out for itself a unique identity and on maintaining that identity at all costs. Its primary author knew the true cost all too well. Michael Sattler was born in Staufen and became a Benedictine monk. The Benedictine Order was one of the oldest, if not the original, monastic orders, established in the sixth century. It stressed brotherly union, repudiating the hierarchy that so marked the Roman Catholic Church.

When Sattler left Roman Catholicism, he would take this idea of brotherly union with him. Right about the time he left the church in 1525, he found himself in Zurich. By June he was baptized, showing that he sided with Grebel over Zwingli. After emerging from his baptismal waters, he quickly became a leader of the group. He was also an outlaw. This band of outlaws managed to hold a synod (a meeting of the church's leaders) at Schleitheim in the cold winter months of 1527.

He was tracked throughout that spring, and by May the forces of Archduke Ferdinand arrested him and brought him to trial at Rottenburg. The list of nine charges included both civil and ecclesiastical crimes. They were read aloud in court on May 15, 1527. Sattler offered a brief reply, but his accusers weren't looking for a debate. "O you infamous, desperate villain and monk, shall we dispute with you? The hangman shall dispute with you, I assure you," the town clerk said. On May 21 he was brutally tortured and then burned at the stake (not hanged as the clerk foretold) at the hands of Roman Catholic and civil authorities. He was followed in martyrdom by his wife who was drowned on May 29.[4]

THE CHARGES AGAINST MICHAEL SATTLER

First, that he and his adherents have acted contrary to the mandate of the Emperor.

Secondly, he has taught, held and believed that the body and blood of Christ are not present in the sacrament.

Thirdly, he has taught and believed that infant baptism does not conduce to salvation.

Fourthly, they have rejected the sacrament of extreme unction [last rites].

Fifthly, they have despised and condemned the Mother of God and the saints.

Sixthly, he has declared that men are not to swear [take oaths] before the authorities.

Seventhly, he has commanded a new and unheard of custom in regard to the Lord's Supper, placing the bread and wine on a plate, and eating and drinking the same.

Eighthly, he has left the [Benedictine] order and married a wife.

Ninthly, he has said that if the Turks [Muslims] should invade the country, no resistance ought to be offered them; and if it were right to wage war, he would rather take the field against the Christians than against the Turks; and it is certainly a great matter, to set the enemies of our holy faith against us.

(Cited in *Martyrs Mirror,* page 416)

In that intervening week between his trial and martyrdom, he was able to send a letter to the brethren at Horb. He admonished them not to grow weary, not to be overcome by opposition, not to waver in the face of suffering and persecution. Instead he urged them to conduct themselves in a godly manner and to remain committed to their beliefs and practices. He then ended with this exhortation: "Look for your Shepherd; he shall give you everlasting rest; for he is nigh at hand that shall come in the end of the world. Be ready of the reward of the kingdom. . . . Flee the shadow of this world." He signed it, "Written in the tower at Binzdorf. Brother Michael Sattler of Staufen, together with my fellow prisoners in the Lord."[5] Michael Sattler is only one of the many Radical Reformers worth taking the time to get to know.

FACES OF THE ANABAPTISTS

If any of the Radical Reformers deserves the title *radical* in terms of extreme behavior and practice, it is Thomas Muentzer (1489–1525). Muentzer is to Luther as Conrad Grebel is to Zwingli, which is to say that Luther's reforms inspired Muentzer, Luther mentored Muentzer, and Luther was viewed as not going far enough in his reforms by Muentzer. At Luther's urging, Muentzer was installed as priest at Zwickau in 1520, a post he managed to hold on to for about a year. After he got to Zwickau, Muentzer quickly parted ways with Luther, advocating radical reforms and rising as one of the leaders in the Peasants' Revolt. Muentzer turned the Reformation into a revolution.

He also held a radical view of prophecy, seeing it as ongoing and seeing himself as a prophet. He was led to believe, through a prophetic vision, he claimed, that the Kingdom of God would reign supreme over all earthly kingdoms, beginning with the ones ruled by the German princes and nobles. Inspired by this belief, he led a meager force into battle at Frankenhausen. His army was defeated, and Muentzer was captured and then beheaded on May 27, 1525. While he held to believer's baptism, linking him with the Anabaptists, his views on church and state and on war clearly marked him off from most of the Anabaptists.

Muentzer's opposite can be found in Menno Simons (1496–1561). After being ordained as a Roman Catholic priest in 1524, Menno lasted about twelve years before he had no choice but to leave his church and form what would come to be a new sect based on Anabaptist principles and a return to following the simple commands of the New Testament Gospels. His followers came to be known as Mennonites, continuing to the present day in large numbers and in a variety of groups. While a priest, Menno—he went by his first name in the Anabaptist spirit of humility—came to disagree with the doctrines of transubstantiation and infant baptism. He also firmly held to the separation of church and state and to pacifism, the principles established in the Schleitheim Confession. He lived mostly in the Rhine regions, though his followers fared better in Switzerland than in the German lands, where they faced intense persecution.

Menno Simons

Menno's conversion to pacifism came after an intense time of soul-searching following his brother's death. His brother had been linked with a group in the town of Munster. They were followers of Thomas Muentzer, who sought to establish a utopian religious community committed to some of the tenets of Anabaptist theology. Pacifism wasn't among them, as they sought to establish their utopia by military means. Despite their self-declared theocratic army, they were sorely defeated, and Menno's brother was killed in the aftermath. Menno cherished the idea of a separatist, almost utopian community, but he also deeply rejected militarism as the means to establish it. Instead he became committed to nonviolence and pacifism. In 1540 he wrote his *Foundation Book*, a blueprint for a communitarian (the holding of goods in common) church governed by the New Testament Gospels and marked by peace.[6]

Martyrdom of Maria von Monjou by Drowning, 1552

Jakob Hutter (? –1536) pursued a similar vision to Menno Simons's in Moravia, modern-day Czech Republic. Originally born in Southern Tirol, now Northern Italy, Hutter held to believer's baptism, pacifism, and communitarianism. He gathered followers, known as the Hutterites. Persecuted in their homelands, the Hutterites eventually made their way to Moravia due to its religious toleration. While journeying to gain converts, Hutter was arrested and was eventually burned at the stake by Roman Catholic officials on February 25, 1536. Such martyrdoms were not unwelcome by most Anabaptists as they allowed them to fully identify with the suffering and persecution of Christ. They also lived in this world rather ambivalently, finding their true home in heaven and in the world to come. Death for them was but the beginning. In fact, their view of martyrdom was but a piece of their larger view of the world altogether.

IN BUT NOT OF

One of the perennial challenges facing the church is that of the church's relationship to culture. Christ set the boundaries when he told his disciples on the eve of his arrest that we are to be in but not of the world (John 17:11-19). Theologians, pastors, and laity have been trying to figure out how to pull that off ever since Christ first spoke those words. In his classic book *Christ & Culture* (1951), H. Richard Niebuhr identified five main responses to this challenge of living in but not of the world, which he calls "the enduring problem." The first he calls *Christ against culture*. This group thinks little of culture or of the world, replacing it entirely with a Christian or spiritual one. On the other end of the spectrum lies the position of *Christ of culture*, which Niebuhr further labels as the accomodationist approach. This group identifies Christianity with a given culture. In the middle of these two extremes are three more approaches: *Christ above culture*, which sets up two different worlds; *Christ and culture in paradox*, which also sets up two different worlds; and *Christ transforming culture*, which sees the Christian community transforming the world by living out its Christian commitment. Niebuhr makes an impassioned plea for Christ transforming culture as the best approach.[7] The Anabaptists, however, would disagree.

Taking Matthew 5–7 as a point of departure for just about all of their theology, the Anabaptists thought that the only proper response to the challenge of living in but not of the world is Christianity against culture.[8] The values of Matthew 5–7 simply don't work in the real world—if someone takes your coat and you give your shirt too, you're just about done for. The Anabaptists, in other words, saw that the only way to live out their Christian commitment was by separating from the world. Eventually they would need to establish their own communities and their own ethical codes and their own value systems. They would truly become a peculiar people. In short, they saw separation as the only surefire way to be *in* but not *of* the world. Christianity is, to borrow Niebuhr's phrase, against culture.

ANABAPTIST BELIEFS

Calvinists have their T-U-L-I-P, and the Anabaptists have their B-A-S-I-N. The Calvinist's T-U-L-I-P represents their beliefs on the doctrines of grace (see Chapter Five). Being the flower of the Netherlands, the acrostic pulls double duty by handily summarizing the doctrines and reminding us of the historical context and location of their formulation. The acrostic B-A-S-I-N also pulls double duty. The letters well represent distinct Anabaptist beliefs and practices, while the basin image symbolizes humility and service as it reminds one of the footwashing practice in the Gospels.

B = Brotherhood of all believers—refuting the hierarchy of Roman Catholicism

A = Adult (or believers') baptism—refuting infant baptism

S = Separation of church and state—revealing a central tenet

I = In the world, but not of it—showing the belief in separation from worldliness

N = Nonviolent resistance—stressing the view of pacifism

The fourth article of the Schleitheim Confession, espousing separation, expresses this view well: "For truly all creatures are but in two classes, good and bad, believing and unbelieving, darkness and light, the world and those who are out of the world, God's temple and idols, Christ and Belial; and none can have part with the other." "The command of the Lord is clear," it concludes. We are called "to be separate." To pull this off, the Anabaptists established their own communities complete with distinct patterns of conduct and dress, visible reminders that they were not part of the world. The followers of Jacob Amman (also spelled Jakob Ammann) are but one such example.

Some of the details of Amman's life are sketchy. Amman was likely born in 1644 (some say it might be as late as 1656), his death occurring sometime before 1730. What we do know for certain is that in the final years of the seventeenth century he led a congregation of Swiss Brethren (a branch of Mennonites), which he was serving as elder, to a stricter adherence to the founding principles of the Radical Reformers.

His congregation emphasized "the ban" in maintaining purity, the second article of the Schleitheim Confession. His followers were called the Amish. They first huddled together in the mountains of Upper Alsace, Switzerland, before making their pilgrimage to William Penn's colony in the New World. Pennsylvania was most appealing, being firmly established on the principle of religious liberty and providing an economic means for their survival as farmers through its rich soils. In this context the Amish would flourish, and they remain there to this day. They are, however, more than a curiosity or a tourist attraction. They are the direct descendants of the Radical Reformers, bent on living in but not of this world, nurturing the values of church, family, land, and community that were the hallmarks of their founders.[9]

Thieleman J. van Braght

MARTYRS MIRROR

The full title of the book by Thieleman J. van Braght, first published in Dutch in 1660, is *The Bloody Theatre, or Martyrs Mirror of the Defenseless Christians, who baptized only upon Confession of Faith, and who suffered and died for the testimony of Jesus, their Savior, from the time of Christ to the year A.D. 1660, compiled from various authentic chronicles, memorials, and testimonies.* Like (John) *Foxe's Book of Martyrs,* with an equally long full title, van Braght started with the apostles and worked his way through the martyrdoms of church history before he told the stories of the contemporary Anabaptist martyrs. He compiled his 1,000-plus-page-book in two parts, Part One taking the reader up to the 1500s and Part Two devoted to the 130-year period of intense persecution of the Anabaptists from their founding in the 1520s until the 1650s. His account overflows with moving stories of spiritual courage in the face of intense opposition. The book remains in print by Herald Press and is especially appreciated by contemporary Anabaptists, reminding them of their heritage and inspiring them in their commitments.

CONCLUSION

From their beginning in Zurich in 1525 to the present day, the Anabaptists or Radical Reformers set out a unique path within Protestantism. They shared much in common with their fellow Reformers. They knew that Roman Catholicism at the end of the Middle Ages had gotten it wrong on so many counts. They knew that the Bible and the gospel had become obscured by centuries of missteps by the church. But they were not at all on the same page with their fellow Reformers in terms of what the new church should look like. Consequently they found themselves smack in the middle of a no-man's-land, with foes on the right and on the left.

Secret Anabaptist Church Service, Amsterdam, 1560s

As contemporary onlookers of the Radical Reformers we may very well find areas of disagreement in theology and church polity and culture. Even contemporary Anabaptist groups have put some distance between themselves and their forebears. Yet, dismissing their contribution both to the Reformation and to the history of the Christian tradition would be quite unwise.

In many ways, the Radical Reformers were like all prophets—despised for challenging the status quo. They were John the Baptists, crying in the wilderness, looking different, and beating out a different message for those who wished to be Christ's disciples. Their way of discipleship is not the only way, and good arguments could be made against some of their beliefs and practices. But their prophetic voice should still be listened to. They had a way of making those who didn't quite see things as they did uncomfortable in their assumptions. This probably more than anything led to their persecution. They still have a way of making onlookers uncomfortable in their assumptions. They are a visible reminder that we should not simply adopt the customs of the world. They remind us that we must think through the impact of culture on our faith and on our church and community. They remind us that ultimate reality is the kingdom of God. And this probably more than anything leads to their contribution both to the Reformation and to the church today.

chapter five

AN OVERNIGHT STAY IN GENEVA

John Calvin and the Swiss Reformation

For how can the thought of God penetrate your mind without
your realizing immediately that, since you are his handiwork . . .
you owe your life to him?

JOHN CALVIN,
THE INSTITUTES OF THE CHRISTIAN RELIGION,
BOOK I, CHAPTER 2.2

When Martin Luther nailed his Ninety-Five Theses to the church door at Wittenberg, a young French student barely took notice. You would think that he would have. Jean Cauvin, the fourth of five sons born to Gerard and Jeanne Cauvin, was supposed to be studying in preparation for ordination and the priesthood. What's more, the theology faculty at his particular college, the College of Montaigu, was tasked by France's ecclesiastical elite to refute Luther and his ideas. Surely they were talking about the renegade German monk in their classes. Yet, all of this was lost on young Jean Cauvin. He was going to be a lawyer, a scholar, a significant figure in the New Learning and the blossoming humanism of France's intelligentsia. His future, he thought, would be in the corridors of academe and in the bookstalls of Paris, not in the pulpit.

That's what he thought. By the end of his life, however, he was in the pulpit, and he was in the city of Geneva—in Switzerland of all places. John Calvin, the English form of his name, was learning firsthand the doctrines he would come to champion so eloquently and persuasively, the doctrines of the sovereignty of God and his gracious hand of providence.

ACTA
SYNODI
NATIONALIS,
In nomine Domini nostri
IESU CHRISTI,

Autoritate

DD. ORDINVM
GENERALIVM FOEDERATI
BELGII PROVINCIARUM,
DORDRECHTI
HABITÆ
Anno CIƆIƆ CXVIII ET CIƆ IƆ CXIX.

Accedunt Plenissima, de Quinque Articulis, Theologorum Iudicia.

DORDRECHTI,
Typis ISAACI IOANNIDIS CANINI,
& Sociorum ejusdem Urbis Typographorum. 1620.
Cum privilegio Ill. Ordd. Generalium.

Acts of the Synod of Dort, 1620

THE FIVE POINTS

If Calvin is known for anything it's his so-called "Five Points," the summary of his doctrines of humanity, sin, and salvation. The actual formation of the "Five Points," however, came after Calvin's death. In the early decades of the 1600s, his followers largely controlled the church in the Netherlands. There was a group, however, who came to part ways with the teaching of Calvin, especially in terms of human nature, the freedom of the will, and the role we play in salvation. This group, following the teaching of Jacobus Arminius, who was led away from Calvin's teaching while preparing to defend Calvinism, formulated the five points of the Remonstrance in 1610. A synod was called at the town of Dordrecht to refute the Remonstrance in 1618–1619. Out of this synod comes the Canons of Dort (or sometimes Dordt—an abbreviated form of the city name of Dordrecht). Much later someone distilled the fifty-page document that is the Canons of Dort into the so-called Five Points, using T-U-L-I-P, the Netherlands' famous flower, as an acrostic.

T = Total depravity, the full and universal depravity of human nature

U = Unconditional election. God's choosing of his own is based on his good pleasure, not on any merit of the creature.

L = Limited atonement. Christ died to secure the salvation of his elect, not simply to provide salvation or to make individuals savable.

I = Irresistible grace. God's calling of individuals to himself cannot be thwarted.

P = Perseverance of the saints. The elect will someday be glorified, their salvation secure.

Calvin is often understood out of context, as if he formed his ideas and established his particular take on doctrine, what we call Calvinism, in utter isolation from other people and cut off from the world around him. The picture most have of Calvin is a lone gun turning ideas over in his head in his ivory tower. This couldn't be further from the truth. Long before the contemporary gurus of church growth started batting around the notion of the church as community, Calvin pioneered it. The church as community was not just simply an idea for him either. His life and his theology depended on it. Also, long before evangelicalism's philosophical pundits began propounding the merits of a distinctly and fully Christian worldview, centuries before in fact, Calvin pioneered this concept too.

Calvin's greatest contribution to the church might very well lie beyond his particular take on the doctrines of grace, the so-called Five

Points of Calvinism. Instead it is squarely located in his labors and love for the church and his equal devotion to a full-orbed submission to the lordship of Christ over every area of life. The proof of one's mettle most often can be seen in his or her followers. Over the centuries those who call themselves Calvinists have made enduring contributions to the Christian tradition in just about every sphere.

They have been in the vanguard of theology—consider the Princeton theologians Charles Hodge and B. B. Warfield. They have been princes of preachers with a heart for evangelism and revival—consider Jonathan Edwards, Charles Spurgeon, and our contemporary John Piper. They have pioneered missions—consider the founder of the modern missions movement, William Carey. They have led the way in philosophy—consider John Witherspoon in the previous era and Alvin Plantinga and Nicholas Wolterstorff in the current one. They have been politicians—consider the Netherlands' Prime Minister Abraham Kuyper. They have been artists and philosophers of art—consider Francis Schaeffer and Hans Rookmaaker. All of these and more share Calvin's devotion to serving God in his church and in his world.

It wasn't, however, just Calvin standing alone in Geneva that started the movement that bears his name. He was surrounded by like-minded colleagues who worked to reform the church, helping it become salt and light in a world of desperate need. We first see this circle of influence impacting Calvin while a student at Paris.

AH, PARIS!

The Reformation came at a glacier's pace to France, and it never enjoyed the upper hand as it had in places such as Germany, the Swiss cantons, and England. France, like Italy and Spain, could never seem to get beyond Roman Catholic domination. There was a minor exception in the royal line at Navarre, an exception that we'll explore in Chapter Eight. While Germany was moving headlong into reform, France lagged woefully behind. Such was the case in Paris in the 1520s when Calvin, as a teenager, was pursuing his academic degrees. Only a handful were entertaining Luther's ideas. Those who adopted them were arrested or driven underground or forced to flee to the hill country. Just prior to taking his Master's degree in 1528 at the age of eighteen—nobody ever accused Calvin of being intellectually dull—he came into contact with one of these who had an affinity for Luther—Jacques Lefevre, a scintillating scholar of the first order.[1]

Calvin, however, veered away from studying theology and preparing for the ministry. He was sent to Paris under a scholarship by his local parish obligating him to return and serve in the church. But a fallout between his father and the church—historians aren't sure exactly what occurred—severed the relationship and released Calvin from his obligation. Calvin turned his energies to studying law and becoming part of Paris's intelligentsia. To signal his presence, he published his first book in 1532, a commentary on the Roman philosopher-jurist Seneca. *Commentary on Lucius Anneas Seneca's Two Books of Clemency* certainly sounds impressive, but it didn't sell at all. Over the next two years Calvin would find his life taking yet another turn as he came under the influence of Nicholas Cop.

Cop served as rector at the Sorbonne, the stronghold of Roman Catholicism in France. Cop, however, shocked everyone when he came out in support of Luther. Through Cop's influence, Calvin eventually left the field of law and left Roman Catholicism. By May 1534 he was converted. Paris proved too volatile an environment as authorities turned up the heat on Reformation sympathizers, forcing Calvin to travel around France. Somehow he managed to publish another book in 1535, the first of what would be many editions of his classic text, *Institutes of the Christian Religion.*[2]

WHY DID CALVIN PREFACE HIS INSTITUTES WITH A LETTER TO A ROMAN CATHOLIC KING?

Calvin prefaced his theological masterpiece, *The Institutes of the Christian Religion*, with a lengthy letter to King Francis I (1494–1547). Not only was France's monarch Roman Catholic, he was actively persecuting Reformers. Calvin hoped the book would show Francis I the sound doctrine of the reformed church and the corrupt doctrine of the Roman Catholic Church. At the very least, Calvin argued that Francis I should put an end to the unjust persecution. While we rightly think of *The Institutes* as a theological text, we need to see that Calvin intended it to be an apologetic text as well.

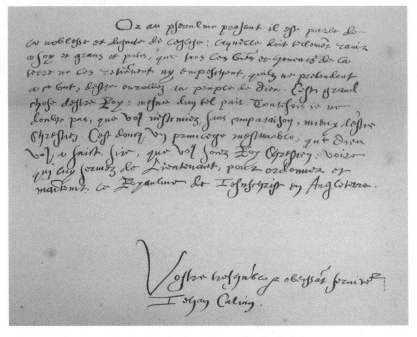

Handwritten Manuscript of John Calvin

A FUNNY THING HAPPENED ON THE WAY TO STRASBOURG

Calvin decided to leave France for the Swiss city of Strasbourg in order to partner with Martin Bucer, a leader of the Reformation in Switzerland. His circuitous journey took him through Geneva where he planned on staying just one night in the home of an old acquaintance from Paris, William Farel. As Calvin prepared to leave the next day, Farel implored him to stay, going so far as to throw in an ultimate threat. "If you refuse," Farel warned, punctuating each syllable with his pointed finger, "God will unquestionably condemn you." Calvin deferred to his wishes. That he believed the unquestionable warning is doubtful; that he was moved by Farel's sincerity is certain. Both Geneva and Calvin would never be the same.

GVILLIELMVS FARELLVS.
*Gallica mirata est Caluinum Ecclesia semper,
Quo nemo docuit doctius.
Est quoque te semper mirata Farelle tonantem
Quo nemo tonuit fortius.*

William Farel

A postcard-picture spot, Geneva nestles against a lake surrounded by mountains. The city could boast inhabitants as far back as the days of Julius Caesar. To this day it is an international city, formerly home to the League of Nations and currently host to a plethora of United Nations agencies and international relief organizations. The International Red Cross was founded there in 1864 and continues to make Geneva its headquarters to this day.

In January 1537, when Calvin and Farel began their work in earnest, Geneva had been catapulted into the throes of change and was still reeling. The city authorities were at a crossroads, having just the prior year thrown out Roman Catholicism, the all-encompassing power for centuries. They were not sure what path to take, and they were certainly not sure about putting their collective futures in the hands of "that Frenchman," as they liked to call Calvin.

CALVIN GETS TO STRASBOURG AFTER ALL

Undeterred by their ambivalence to him, Calvin pushed hard and fast for reform. He would have done better with some soft-pedaling. By 1538 the town authorities voted him out of the church and out of the town. Calvin once again wandered. He first went to Basel. Then his old

75

friend Martin Bucer invited him to Strasbourg to pastor a congregation of French refugees. This was no small church, numbering over four hundred. Among the parishioners was a widow, Idelette de Bure. Calvin had previously known her and her family, having debated her husband who had Anabaptist leanings before Calvin convinced him otherwise. In addition to marrying Idelette and preaching almost daily, Calvin returned to writing, producing the first of what would come to be his many commentaries and books of sermons.

Meanwhile, back in Geneva things were unraveling rather quickly. The Roman Catholic Church wanted to regain control of the city, and the vacuum of leadership at the church was making the prospects for such a return look all too real. The town authorities went to Calvin hat in hand, pleading for his return. Calvin was reluctant. "There is no place under heaven that I am more afraid of," he was heard to say. But he went back, a married man and a man on a mission.

CALVIN AS CHURCHMAN

B. B. Warfield, the so-called lion of Princeton, dubbed Calvin the theologian of the Holy Spirit. Warfield was trying to point out that Calvin's overlooked achievement was his thought on the Holy Spirit. With all due deference to Warfield, I'd like to dub Calvin the theologian of the church, as it seems he is equally overlooked in his thought on the church. Contemporary Protestants might be aghast to hear that Calvin once said, agreeing with church father Cyprian, that "For those to whom [God] is Father the church may also be Mother."[3] His quote, in fact, sounds far too Romish, especially for the liking of contemporary American evangelicals. His quote nevertheless is one that we, especially contemporary American evangelicals, need to pause over for a moment.

In today's Christian environment we can live our entire Christian lives from start to finish without ever passing through a church door. There's Christian radio, Christian television, even entire Christian satellite networks, and many Christian sites on the Web. There are evangelistic crusades and rallies in stadiums. There are Christian bookstores and Christian magazines. Not to mention the ascendancy of parachurch organizations in the current Christian culture. Everything you need for the

Christian life can be had without ever entering a church. Such realities would surely grieve Calvin. He simply couldn't conceive of Christianity without the church. He couldn't think of living the Christian life without being rooted in and connected to the local church.

CALVIN'S CHURCH

Unlike Luther, no denomination bears John Calvin's name; yet his influence extends directly to many denominations and indirectly to others still. His impact on Knox, as well as Knox's own thought, may be seen behind Presbyterianism. Various churches who take the name Reformed may also trace their roots to Calvin, such as the Christian Reformed Church or the Dutch Reformed Church. His thought underlies both The Westminster Standards (1647) and The Thirty-Nine Articles (1559), the doctrinal confession of the Anglican Church. His name may not be part of a denomination, but Calvinism represents a rather large group of people who subscribe in varying degrees to the five points that summarize his teaching on the doctrines of grace.

Not everything Calvin did for the church has been seen as positive. Holding to what has come to be called the "regulative principle," which holds that if it is not explicitly mentioned in the Bible it should not be done, Calvin did away with musical instruments. Instruments were clearly part of the worship of the saints of the Old Testament era, but they were absent in the worship of the saints in the New Testament churches. Calvin also believed that the only songs to be sung in the church were the words of Scripture themselves. Here he did look to the Old Testament. Calvin took the position of exclusive psalmody, believing that only the Psalms should be sung in church.

Calvin's argument against Paul's injunctions to sing "psalms and hymns and spiritual songs" (Eph. 5:19; Col. 3:16) interprets the final two clauses in apposition to the first. That's simply grammar-speak to say that the verse better reads as "psalms, which are hymns and spiritual songs." While that's a grammatically possible interpretation, whether it's the right interpretation is another question. John Knox picked up on this view of Calvin while he was in exile in Geneva during the reign of Bloody Mary (see Chapter Six) and imbued Presbyterianism, at least in its fledgling years, with the view of exclusive psalmody. In fact, until the days of Isaac Watts (1674–1748) and Charles and John Wesley (1707–1788 and 1703–1791 respectively), founders of English hymnody, English Protestants were by and large exclusively psalm singers, revealing the extent of Calvin's reach.

Of course, this particular view of music set Calvin off from Luther, who was as good a musician as he was a theologian. Luther was writing hymns for the German church long before Isaac Watts appeared on the scene of the English church. Calvin and Luther did agree on many things, however. Topping that list would have to be the marks of the true church. On this they were on the same page. Luther and Calvin never met, but they did exchange letters. In one letter Calvin wrote, "Would that I could fly to you, that I might even for a few hours enjoy the happiness of your society . . . but seeing that it is not granted to us on earth, I hope that shortly it will come to pass in the kingdom of God."[4]

If they had gotten together, you can safely bet that they would have been talking about the church. The discussion of the true marks of the church was a vital one in the Reformation era. In fact, it had everything to do with the Reformation. The Roman Catholic Church claimed to be the true church by default. The Reformers held up a different standard. You couldn't prove to be the true church, Calvin said, just by claiming to be the true church. You need evidence. Calvin and Luther pointed to the telltale sign, the watertight evidence, of the true church: the preaching of the Word. This was paramount to both of them, for only in the Word do we find the gospel, and the gospel is the church's true treasure, something Luther was saying from the time he nailed his Ninety-Five Theses to the church door.

The Word is God's gift to his church. He has promised to bless it. Only where the Word is central may one find the true church. In addition to the preaching of the Word as the mark of the true church, Calvin added the sacraments as well. Of course, he only held to the two sacraments of baptism and the Lord's Supper, over and against the seven sacraments practiced by the Roman Catholic Church. Calvin saw the sacraments in the same way he saw the Word—God's gifts for the church, intended as means of grace and blessing for his people.

When John Knox took Calvin's ideas back with him to Scotland, he added a third mark—church discipline. What Knox was really doing was simply making explicit what Calvin thought implicitly. Calvin took Paul's injunction regarding the Lord's Supper seriously and strongly implored his congregation not to partake if they were unworthy of doing so (1 Cor. 11:27). We also, in the middle of all this church discipline talk, need to remember Calvin's own injunction to be gracious. "There would be no church," he once said, "if we set a standard of absolute perfection, for the best of us are still far from the ideal."[5]

LOCKING THE DOORS

Despite his insistence on the primacy of the church, Calvin knew the church had its limits. John Bunyan's *Pilgrim's Progress* illustrates these limits well. We'll see this in Chapter Seven more fully, but in his classic allegory Bunyan calls the church "The house built by the Lord of the Hill for the safety and rest of pilgrims." Bunyan has his main character, Christian, enter this house, the church; he has him "fed," his allegory for the sermon and for the Lord's Supper; and he has him led into the armory, where he is equipped. Then Bunyan has the keepers of the house send him away, out into the world. Calvin did the same for his parishioners by locking the church doors after the service. Christians, having been fed and equipped, refreshed and nourished, are to be in the world, according to Calvin.

Theologians of the medieval era tended to downplay life outside the walls of the church or monastery or convent. They tended to give little credence to one's work in the world and to the world itself. Calvin and Luther, joined by many other Reformers, hammered out a doctrine of vocation: one's work is a calling. They also reminded their congregations and us that this is God's world, and we are to cultivate it and enjoy it for God's glory. Calvin locked the church doors so the church could be in the world.

The city of Geneva is clear testament to his view. Its current status as a humanitarian center for the world has much to do with Calvin and his legacy. Under his leadership the city promoted laws that supported the family, outlawing spousal abuse and elevating marriage as an institution. His sphere of leadership also extended to cleaning up the streets, with laws against public drunkenness and public disorderly conduct. On the positive side, hospitals were built and the entire education system overhauled. A "no child left behind" policy was truly enacted, seeing that all of Geneva's children had an education.

Those who know about Calvin, however, may know something that doesn't set right with this rosy picture of Calvin and his humanitarianism—Calvin and Geneva ordered the death of Servetus. His crime? He held an unorthodox view of the Trinity. Calvin's part in this, as well as the whole Servetus affair itself, needs to be qualified. First, Servetus came to Geneva having escaped from Roman Catholic authorities who had already condemned him for his beliefs. Only two heresies were punishable by death according to the law of the Holy Roman Empire—heresies related to the Trinity and the insistence on believers' baptism (in place of infant baptism). If Geneva let Servetus, who was bent on spreading his views that Christ was not God, go, the fledgling reformed church would be seen as taking a lesser stance on heretics than the Catholics were willing to take. Further, Calvin didn't condemn or put Servetus to death—the town council did. It is true, however, that if he had wanted to, Calvin could have stopped them from doing it.

While these qualifications may help us better understand the context of the Servetus affair, they do not excuse Calvin or the city of Geneva from its heinous action in executing him. Calvin was wrong. It's just unfortunate that this event so clouds Calvin in many contemporary perspectives. We can't make excuses for him. Neither, however, should we dismiss him for it.

Calvin's legacy, though tainted by the Servetus affair, far outshines it. This can be clearly seen in the legacy of worldview thinking that stems from his thought. While Calvin believed in the depravity of human nature—that all humans are born with a sin nature—he also believed in the dignity of human nature. We are, Calvin liked to say again and again, born in the image of God, our Creator. Though it is difficult to hold these twin principles of depravity and dignity in tension, Calvin did. He was aware of humanity's potential and achievements, all the while being aware of humanity's limitations and frailties. Further, while Calvin knew that the Kingdom of God was not of this world, he also knew that this world was created by God and was to be enjoyed and was to be a means for glorifying God.

Theodore Beza

CALVIN'S LEGACY: THEODORE BEZA

Calvin had many students and followers, but his true understudy and successor was Theodore Beza (1516–1605). Beza was born in the Burgundy region of France and, like Calvin, studied law and humanities at the University of Orleans before eventually making his way to Geneva. Calvin had him installed as head of the Academy. Upon Calvin's death, Beza was appointed moderator of the Company of Pastors (*Compagnie des Pasteurs*) in Geneva. He led further reforms of the church, cementing Calvin's ideas and views, being a formidable theologian and churchman. He was in fact quite a versatile scholar, publishing an edition of the Greek New Testament (1582) and teaming up with Calvin to produce a French translation of the New Testament. He even produced a work of church history that offered brief biographies of the Reformers, most of whom he knew personally. Like Calvin, he also longed to see freedom for Protestants in France, his home country. He made frequent trips to France on behalf of the Reformation cause. He even dedicated one of his books, a prayer book, to England's Elizabeth I in the hopes of enlisting her support for the beleaguered French reformers.

This view of the world led Calvin to stress the value of work and the value of life in the world. He gave new meaning to raising families and to earning a living at work. He further held that we are bound to the creation or cultural mandate in Genesis 1:26-28 to subdue the earth. Calvin viewed the creation mandate as a call for humanity to cultivate the earth as stewards of God's creation. His views on this have led to the rich legacy of Calvinism in the arts, politics, and worldview thinking. Calvin locked the church doors after the service because he wanted the church to be salt and light in the world that God made and entrusted to us.

CONCLUSION

The year 2009 will mark the five hundredth year since Calvin's birth. His ideas are as hotly debated as ever, finding both adherents and detractors. While not all may agree with him, it is difficult to discredit the role he has played in both the Reformation and in the history of the Christian tradition. Though no denomination bears his name, he has left his mark on numerous churches. His *Institutes of the Christian Religion* remains widely used as a textbook in theology and as a means for leading the faithful into deeper reflections on God and his work in his world. Calvin marked off the boundaries for the discussion of the doctrines of humanity, sin, and salvation even up to the present day. He also labored for the church, leaving behind a rich legacy for generations already past and to come.

CALVIN'S WRITINGS

Calvin's most famous work is the *Institutes of the Christian Religion*. It was first published in 1535, just about a year after his conversion. He revised and enlarged it throughout his lifetime, taking the original from six chapters to seventy-nine. The last edition, the one that is mostly read today, was published in 1559 in both Latin and French. He also produced commentaries on over half of the books of the Old Testament and all of the books of the New Testament except Revelation. Additionally, his published sermon series include the books of Ephesians, Romans, and Hosea. He wrote many, many tracts and minor treatises addressing particular problems in the church or specific theological issues. His immense correspondence has been published in English, filling four volumes.

IN OMNES PAVLI A-
postoli Epistolas, atque etiam in
Epistolam ad Hebræos, item in
Canonicas Petri, Iohannis, Iaco-
bi, & Iudæ, quæ etiam Catholicæ
vocantur,

IOH. CALVINI COMMENTARII.

Hanc Commentariorum postremam esse recognitionem, ex lectione atque
collatione cum prioribus, deprehendet lector.

Oliua Roberti Stephani.
.M. D. LVI.

Calvin's Commentary on New Testament Epistles, 1556

Calvin and Idellete had but one child, a son who died shortly after birth. Calvin also buried his wife. Both events, as we will see more fully in Chapter Eight, nearly sent him off the edge. Though without a literal posterity, Calvin's sons and daughters in the faith are truly incalculable. When English Protestants were forced into exile during the brutal reign of Bloody Mary, most of them made their way to Geneva. When they returned, they took what they heard Calvin teach and what they saw him do in Geneva back with them. It's not too much of a stretch to say that most Puritan thought and practice is owing to Calvin. His large congregations at Strasbourg and Geneva were nurtured in the faith as they sat under his preaching. Hundreds of students sat under his teaching at Geneva's Academy. Most of them had sneaked into Geneva from France. Once trained, they went back, risking their very lives to pastor underground churches. These missionary students took the gospel not only into France but all over Europe. A couple of his students even made it to the shores of South America—and this was in the 1500s.

And, of course, we need to mention his writings. His *Institutes*, his various commentaries and sermons, and his letters and other works all continue to be standard fare in seminary reading, having been used in the training of the church's leaders and read by the faithful in the pew for centuries. Calvin has quite a legacy. The five hundredth anniversary of his birth is certainly not to go unnoticed, nor should it.

chapter six

A KING AND A DIVORCE

The Anglicans and the British Reformation

> ... Be it enacted, by authority of this present Parliament, that the king, our sovereign lord, his heirs and successors, kings of this realm, shall be taken, accepted, and reputed the only supreme head in earth of the church in England, called Anglicans Ecclesia.
>
> ACT OF SUPREMACY, 1534

Germany had Luther. Switzerland had Zwingli and Calvin and Grebel. England had a king. Henry VIII, truly larger than life, was already on his second wife and was desperately seeking a male heir. They had six children, but only one survived, a daughter, Mary. For this, Henry sought to have the marriage annulled. The only problem was that his wife, Catherine, was the niece of the Holy Roman Emperor, and the emperor pressured the pope not to allow the English monarch to shame his family. Henry pressed for the annulment anyway. When his Lord Chancellor, Thomas Wolsey, failed to secure one, Henry had him sacked for treason.

In Wolsey's place came Thomas Cranmer, whom Henry appointed Archbishop of Canterbury. Cranmer, desirous of theological reform, counseled Henry to break with the church of Rome. To set the wheels in motion, Cranmer himself annulled the marriage, leading the way for Henry to marry Anne Boleyn, with whom he'd been having an affair. Rome retaliated by excommunicating Henry. Henry then delivered the final blow in the contest. In 1534 Henry and Parliament declared the Act of Supremacy. In England the king, not the pope in Rome, would be the head of the church. The Reformation had come, albeit like the plot of a soap opera, to England.

IN THE RIGHT PLACE AT THE RIGHT TIME

The figure that garnishes all of the attention is Henry VIII. The true reformer, however, was his archbishop, Thomas Cranmer. Cranmer's story is a bit out of place. In England in the sixteenth century, with its system of landed gentry and nobility by birthright, rags to riches stories were scarce, let alone stories of those who rose from humble beginnings to have the king's ear. But this was the story of Thomas Cranmer.

Born in 1489 in an obscure village to a family with little means, Cranmer rose through his intellectual rigor. Distinguishing himself at Jesus College, Cambridge, Cranmer was appointed a fellow in 1510. He was a scholar of the first order and seemed to be headed for a life of quiet reflection among the ivory-covered stone walls of Cambridge's colleges. A rash of sickness hit the placid town in 1529, forcing Cranmer to take an extended holiday in Essex where he met with two of Henry VIII's advisors. As was typical, he left an impression, triggering a series of events that culminated in Cranmer's leaving behind his life in the academy for a life of intrigue in the castle.

By 1533, when Wolsey's failure disappointed Henry, Cranmer was moved into the position of top theological and ecclesiastical advisor to the king. Henry was no slouch himself when it came to theology. He had refuted Luther, or so he thought, in his book *The Defense of the Seven Sacraments* (1521). Pope Leo X, anxious to have supporters in his fight with Luther, heaped praise on Henry's little treatise, granting its author the title "Defender of the Faith." Henry may have written some of it, since he had been working on a refutation of Luther since 1518. Much of the book, however, was most likely written by Thomas More. Henry, nevertheless, knew what he was doing when it came to theology and the church.

It soon became clear to Cranmer, however, that Henry, theologian that he was, was only going to reform the church so far, and not nearly far enough for Cranmer's liking. Henry did begin his program of the dissolution of the monasteries. On the surface his dissolving the monasteries indicated he was serious about ridding England of Catholicism. But under the surface Henry was much more interested in filling his treasury and making friends among the barons and nobles, not to mention picking up a few nice estates for himself. By the 1500s the Roman Catholic Church held large tracts of land with productive farms and forests. The proceeds of the dissolution sale, even at bargain basement prices, made Henry and England very rich and gave a whole new base of power—in the form of land holdings—to a whole new generation of nobility that would be beholden to, and some even beheaded by, Henry.

In reality, while the Act of Supremacy made allegiance to the pope a capital offense and the dissolution of the monasteries appeared to be a step in removing Catholicism from the land, in many places in England Roman Catholicism flourished and held sway. Further, while the hierarchy of the church changed, by and large the king merely replaced the pope. There were still many needed reforms in the church. Cranmer did what he could, but serving under Henry, the amount that he could do always had its limits. So he waited.

ENGLAND'S KINGS AND QUEENS SCORECARD

King Henry VIII		Edward VI	Lady Jane Grey	Mary I
1509–1547		1547–1553	1553	1553–1558
Catholic, then Anglican		Anglican	Anglican	Catholic
Elizabeth I	James I	Charles I	Oliver Cromwell (*Lord Protector*)	Charles II
1558–1603	1603–1625	1625–1649	1649–1658	1660–1685
Anglican	Anglican	Anglican	Puritan/Independent	Anglican

HENRY AND HIS WIVES AND HIS CHILDREN

The marriage to Anne Boleyn failed to measure up to the king's expectations. In other words, no son was born. The only surviving child was another daughter, Elizabeth. Cranmer was called in to annul another marriage, and Anne was then beheaded on the grounds inside the Tower of London. Next came the marriage to Jane Seymour, who did have a son, Edward. By all accounts Henry loved Jane. But she died in giving birth to Edward. Next came Anne of Cleeves. Henry had never met her, having only seen a portrait. When he did see her, after the ceremony, he changed his mind. Another annulment followed. Then came Catherine Howard, who rather unwisely had affairs of her own. Henry had her tried for treason and beheaded. He then married Catherine Parr in 1543. Quite spunky, she managed to outlive him.

The state of the Reformation in Britain for the next fifty years depended entirely on Henry's three surviving children: Edward, Mary, and Elizabeth. When Henry died in 1547, his young and sickly son came to the throne. Among his illnesses was syphilis, which he had contracted in birth. He took the name Edward VI when he ascended to the throne, though he was popularly called England's Josiah, a reference to the young and godly, not to mention wisely counseled, king in Judah (2 Kings 23). With Edward VI on the throne, Cranmer emerged from the shadows. Now was his, and England's, chance for true reform. Cranmer's time of waiting was over.

Edward VI and Mary

Cranmer first set about reforming the church service, taking aim at worship and preaching. He revised the *Book of Common Prayer*, designed for the church's liturgy, and wrote his *Homilies*, written sermons to be preached in pulpits across the breadth of England coinciding with the church calendar. We'll come back to these two documents later. Next Cranmer set his sights on the theology of the church, drafting a new confession of faith, which consisted of a series of articles. The first version had forty-two articles. He was just about to get them passed through the church and Parliament when Edward died in 1553. Cranmer's articles were put on hold. In fact, all of the efforts at reform were frozen. Soon, under Mary, they would all be reversed, and England would return to the fold of the church of Rome.

FROM THE HALLS OF POWER TO THE CHAMBERS OF THE TOWER

Mary had a deep and abiding memory. She was the daughter of Catherine of Aragon, Henry's first wife. She remembered what mockery was made of her mother, and she remembered full well the part that Cranmer played in that. She also was deeply devoted to her Catholicism. It would be her divine errand, so she thought, to rid England of the Protestant heretics, restoring the true church in Rome to its rightful place in England. Cranmer and his followers were unceremoniously taken from their positions of power and deposited in the dark chambers of the Tower of London, where they awaited their martyrdoms on the block or at the stake.

Mary's rise to power was not immediate, however. Knowing that Mary was the rightful heir to the throne, and knowing that she would take the country right back into Catholicism, a group of nobles tried futilely to put fifteen-year-old Lady Jane Grey on the throne. Her reign lasted all of nine days. She too was sent to the Tower, and she too lost her life at the hands of Mary.

In 1554 Mary issued a series of injunctions, declaring "with all speed and diligence" the reversal of the reforms of Henry and Edward. From the Archbishop right on down to the parish priests, all were to be Roman Catholic. Protestant scholars lost their appointments at England's universities, Protestant clergy were ousted and were arrested or went into exile, and Protestant government officials either partook of the Roman sacrament or were dismissed. At Westminster Abbey, the Roman Catholic Mass was celebrated for the first time in twenty years.

For her deeds as England's monarch, history has dubbed her "Bloody Mary." After her death and with the explicit intention that the martyrs during her reign not be forgotten, John Foxe commemorated the lives and sacrifice of those whose blood she spilt. Among the many heroes whose stories are told in *Foxe's Book of Martyrs* are Latimer and Ridley, the so-called Oxford martyrs.

FOXE'S BOOK OF MARTYRS

The full title of the classic text by John Foxe (1516–1587) is *The Actes and Monuments of These Latter and Perillous Days, Touching Matters of the Church.* Popularly, it's referred to as *Foxe's Book of Martyrs.* Foxe was Oxford-educated and served as a private tutor to numerous families during the reigns of Henry VIII and Edward VI. He went into exile under Bloody Mary, first to Germany and then to Basel. While in exile, he embarked on a study of church history, gathering material on Christian martyrs from the first century on. In 1559 he returned to London and began poring over the public records of the Marian persecutions. Others, hearing of his project, sent him records and documents of the many martyrs during Mary's bloody reign. He published the first edition in 1563, and he continued to publish enlarged editions right up to his death in 1587, the final edition reaching nearly 2,500 pages. Most of the reprints today are abridged editions. His book begins with the persecution of the apostles and travels through the centuries. The lion's share of the book, however, is the martyrdoms occurring between 1553 and 1558. *Foxe's Book of Martyrs,* as it is popularly called, has clearly secured its place as a classic text in both the Christian tradition and in British literature.

In the middle of Broad Street in the university town of Oxford, the modern pavement gives way to a collage of centuries-old stone with a cross formed in the center. This monument marks the very spot where Bishops Hugh Latimer and Nicholas Ridley were burned at the stake on October 16, 1555. Ridley came to adopt Reformation principles through the influence of Cranmer, having been a student of his at Cambridge. Edward VI appointed him Bishop of Rochester. Latimer was an Oxford man who, under Edward's reign, was appointed Bishop of Worcester. Both were arrested when Mary ascended the throne. During their trial, they rejected both papal authority and the Roman Mass. For these offenses, they were condemned. While the flames licked their bodies, Latimer famously said to his colleague, "Be of good comfort, Mr. Ridley, and play the man. We shall this day light a candle by God's grace, in England, as I trust never shall be put out."

Cranmer met a similar fate, although he wavered in the face of persecution. He sent a letter expressing his submission to Mary; he doggedly believed in submission to the monarch and to the Roman Church. But Mary thought him disingenuous in his submission and ordered him to be burned at the stake at Oxford. She was bent on revenging the shame Cranmer had brought to her mother, Catherine of Aragon, through his counsel to Henry VIII. Cranmer's impending death brought a clarity and resolve to his true beliefs and commitments. At the very end he reneged his submission to Rome and affirmed his Protestant and Reformed understanding of the gospel. When the fire was lit on the stake, he put his hand into the fire first, exclaiming, "I have sinned, in that I signed with my hand what I did not believe with my heart."

John Foxe wrote his book so the heroic deeds of Ridley, Latimer, Cranmer, and many others would not be forgotten, so their testimonies would inspire Christians whether facing persecution or the temptation not to be steadfast in their commitment to Christ. The prayer commemorating the examples of these three martyrs from the Anglican prayer book puts it eloquently: "Keep us, O Lord, constant in faith and zealous in witness, after the examples of thy servants Hugh Latimer, Nicholas Ridley, and Thomas Cranmer; that we may live in thy fear, die in your favor, and rest in your peace."

Meanwhile, Mary had her own troubles to deal with. She sought a Catholic husband with whom she could have a Catholic heir, securing the throne in that ecclesiastical direction. She married Philip, son of Charles V, Holy Roman Emperor. He, however, found little interest in Mary, returning to his home in Spain after the wedding and only visiting her once in 1557 for political reasons as England and Spain arranged to wage war against France. England lost, and Mary, as those around her would testify, lost the will to live. Her reign of terror against Protestants came to an end in 1558 when she was buried in Westminster Abbey next to her half-sister Elizabeth.

Henry's last surviving child, Elizabeth, was next in line for the throne.

In 1559 she signed yet another Act of Supremacy, declaring England once again free of Roman Catholicism. She reinstated Cranmer's *Book of Common Prayer* and revived the discussion of his articles of theology. His original forty-two were edited down a bit. The last three, expressing strong anti-Anabaptist sentiments, were suppressed. In 1563 the Queen and Parliament adopted the Thirty-Nine Articles as the official confession of faith of the Anglican Church.

Elizabeth's theological reforms, however, were not welcomed by everyone. A number of Protestants thought that Elizabeth, like her father, Henry VIII, had not gone far enough in reforming the doctrine and practice of the church. For one thing, she disliked preaching, going as far as to say on one occasion that two or three preachers should be enough for the whole country. She opted for the ritual that the *Book of Common Prayer* had to offer. She also seemed to fail to grasp the true theological nature of the reforms of Cranmer. Further, she even seemed to placate those who had Romish tendencies. None of this sat well with the "Puritans," those people who desired a pure church, deeply and truly reformed. Elizabeth countered by signing into law the Act of Uniformity (1559). This demanded, under penalty of law, conformity to the Anglican Church. Later she would sign the Act Against the Puritans (1593). This law left no mistaking her distaste for the Puritans. The story of the Puritans is Act Two of the British Reformation and will be taken up in the next chapter.

PRAYERS FOR GOING OUT TO SEA

Cranmer and other Anglican Reformers not only inspire us in their martyrdoms, they also instruct us through their contributions while they lived and worked for the reform of the church. We mentioned earlier in this chapter that three main documents reveal the heart of the British Reformation and Anglicanism: *The Book of Common Prayer*, *The Homilies*, and The Thirty-Nine Articles.

The Thirty-Nine Articles remains the doctrinal confession for Anglicanism. It is Calvinistic on the doctrines of grace and promotes an episcopal (from the Greek word *episcopos*, meaning "bishop") form of church government. A selection from the Thirty-Nine Articles appears in the Appendix.

This theological document has quite a political context, being a significant piece of the so-called Elizabethan Settlement. After the tumultuous years of Mary, Elizabeth was anxious to get things back in order, especially since her empire was threatened by Spain. Eventually England would defeat the Spanish Armada in 1588. The British fleet was helped by a dead, windless sea that delayed the Spanish sailing ships from landing upon England's shores, leaving the Spanish Armada vulnerable as it drifted at sea. Anglican churches across the land rang out with prayers of thanksgiving for the victory over the enemy. Elizabeth, it was said, rode a horse up the steps of one of her palaces in celebration.

That was 1588. Back in 1559, however, the Spanish defeat was far off the horizon, and Elizabeth could little afford a religiously divided country when so much was at stake. To "settle" the religious question, she bargained with Parliament. The Thirty-Nine Articles and a revised *Book of Common Prayer* were the result. Everyone was satisfied. Everyone, that is, except the Puritans.

What Does Church Government Have to Do with It?
Independents, Presbyterians, and Anglicans

While the Reformers in Great Britain shared much in common, they also had their differences, among them the form of church government. Three main responses to the Roman Catholic form emerged in England. The Anglicans espoused an episcopalian form of church government, from the Greek word *espiscopos*, meaning "bishop." This view stressed hierarchy and a centralized base of power, with an archbishop over bishops who were in turn over the clergy. The Presbyterians, from the Greek word *presbyteros*, meaning "elder," stressed a broader base of power in the hands of the presbytery, which consisted of a group of churches in geographical proximity. These various presbyteries formed the General Assembly. Individual congregations were run by the session, consisting of teaching elders (pastors) and ruling elders. The Independents, or Congregationalists, stressed the autonomy of the local congregation, though they would often form decision-making associations among independent congregations.

The revision of *The Book of Common Prayer* adopted by Elizabeth's Parliament is largely the 1552 version that Cranmer got passed under

Edward VI, with one telling change. The Lord's Supper would be now referred to as containing the "real presence" of Christ in the elements. *The Homilies*, which through Cranmer's work had strong language on justification by faith alone, were also modified. Some scholars see in this Elizabeth's nod to Roman Catholics, who had been invigorated by Mary's reign. These concessions did not satisfy all of England's religious factions, especially many of the Puritans. The dissenters could only protest so much, however, since Elizabeth was after all the queen.

Despite their entanglement in politics, *The Book of Common Prayer* and *The Homilies* are truly theological works of art. The prayer book is more than a liturgy for the church service. It offers prayers for every area of life, which is to say it becomes a training manual for living theologically. This is most obvious in the prayers for going out to sea. Sea travel in the sixteenth century was dangerous, to say the least. Navigational equipment was elementary, travel depended entirely upon winds and favorable currents, and the threat of piracy always seemed to lurk. Consequently, the prayer book offers prayers for going out to sea, committing one to God's providence at the start of a voyage. There are even prayers to use during storms at sea—a longer one for more tepid storms and a short one for more urgent occasions. In times of the latter, the bare minimum of words—"Help, Lord, have mercy upon us"—suffice.

There were also prayers for going out to battle. The psalmist's cries to God to smite his enemies provided a good template for these. There were prayers for births and deaths, for the dawn of a new day and for its close as the sun set. In sum, all of life could be and should be a matter of prayer. Today's evangelicals, especially in an American context, have shied away from written prayers, being too afraid of formalism. There is something, however, to these theologically rich and thought-out prayers that should not be so readily dismissed.

American evangelicals also tend to shy away from reading printed sermons from the pulpit, especially those written by someone else (in academic circles such practice is called plagiarism). But in addition to writing out the liturgy and prayers in *The Book of Common Prayer*, Cranmer and others also wrote sermons or homilies for pulpits across England. Cranmer knew the preaching abilities of most of England's clergy to be woefully not up to the task. Right up until the Reformation, the Mass was the church service, and preaching was rarely, if ever, done. Luther faced the same problem with former Roman Catholic ministers who were now Reformed in Germany's pulpits. He, too, took to writing sermons to help them get on their feet.

Cranmer not only feared the lack of good preachers, he also wanted to see that the twin Reformation principles of *Sola Scriptura* and *Sola Fide* would become deeply embedded in the Anglican Church. For these reasons he wrote his *Homilies*, numbering twelve in all and first published in 1547. The first five deal with bedrock doctrines such as justification by faith. The last seven treat issues of the Christian life. In the earlier doctrinal sermons on salvation, faith, and good works, Cranmer declares, "This is the ordinance of God, that they which believe in Christ should be saved without works, by faith only, freely receiving remission of their sins. . . . What can be spoken more plainly, than to say, that freely without works, by faith only, we obtain remission of our sins?"[1] For his homily on Scripture, see the Appendix.

Taken together, The Thirty-Nine Articles, *The Homilies*, and *The Book of Common Prayer* show that, at least in Cranmer's hands, the Reformation in Britain was more than window dressing. Henry VIII may have simply replaced the pope with himself, and Elizabeth I may have been more interested in securing England's political prosperity than its religious one. Nevertheless, under these monarchs the Reformation principles began to make their mark in England. This can especially be seen to the north in Scotland.

MEANWHILE, BACK IN SCOTLAND . . .

Until the time of King James I in the first decade of the 1600s, England and Scotland were not a united kingdom. Before he was king in England, he had been king in Scotland for thirty-six years. There he was King James VI. This gets a little confusing, but the two titles represent one person. James united the kingdoms, largely to secure Great Britain's future. Consequently, the story of the Reformation in Scotland prior to 1603 and the beginning of his joint reign runs a parallel but unique path to that of the Reformation in England.

The most significant figure in the Scottish Reformation is the vivid if not fiery John Knox. Much of Knox's early life is shrouded in mystery.

His date of birth is given as 1513 or 1514, with some accounts claiming 1505, though the earliest date seems unlikely. Scholars are not even sure where he attended college. What is known is that by the early 1540s Knox was ordained as a Roman Catholic priest. Henry VIII's Act of Supremacy (1534) did not extend the Reformation to Scotland. Sometime after 1544 Knox came into contact with George Wishart, a wholehearted convert to Reformation principles. Wishart was burned at the stake in 1546. Wishart's other followers retaliated by murdering Cardinal Beaton, Scotland's supreme Catholic official. For nearly a year those espousing Reformed principles made some headway in Scotland from their base at the castle at St. Andrews. With the help of French forces, Catholics regained the upper hand, taking the castle and sending its Protestant inhabitants, John Knox among them, to the galley ships as prisoners.

John Knox

Knox spent eighteen long months in the most dire circumstances, rowing about as a prisoner. In 1549 he was released, and he set to work reforming the church in Scotland. Mary's ascent to the throne sent John Knox, and many others, into exile. He arrived in Geneva in September 1554. His time there with Calvin would have a lasting impact on him and on his beloved Scotland, to which he returned in 1556 only to leave again that same year, heading back to the safer environs of Geneva.

Knox returned to Scotland a second time in 1559 determined to do for his country what Calvin had done for the city of Geneva. Knox thought Calvin's Geneva to be "the most perfect school of Christ there ever was on earth." Knox would try to have the same said of his Scotland. By 1560 Knox established Presbyterianism as the national Church of Scotland. In his *Book of Discipline* (1560), he famously lays out the three marks of the true church: preaching of the Word, the proper practice of the two sacraments, and church discipline. The dissolution of the monasteries in Scotland brought a flow of money into the national treasuries. Through Knox's influence and leadership, such monies were used for a massive educational campaign, resulting in an almost entirely literate country—the first such achievement for any nation in history. To his list of accomplishments, Knox is also credited as the founder of Presbyterianism.

Knox also managed to run himself aground with the monarchs due largely to his book *The First Blast of the Trumpet Against the Monstrous Regiment of Women* (1558), aimed at Bloody Mary, Elizabeth I, and Mary of Guise, queen in Scotland. At one time Mary of Guise called him the most dangerous man in her entire realm, feeling not a little threatened by his attacks on her Catholicism. After leading the church in Scotland for just over a decade, Knox died in 1572. Contemporary chroniclers point out that a car park, as the British say—a parking garage—has been built over his grave near the church of St. Giles. Pilgrims wishing to pay homage to Scotland's Reformer may do so at space number 66.

CONCLUSION

The British Reformation was truly a roller coaster ride, following the predilections of the given monarch. It had its ups and downs over the decades, even centuries, of its makings. As will be seen in the next chapter, this roller coaster ride also produced a far more versatile Protestantism than any of the other Reformation movements. Luther and his fellow Germans produced Lutheranism, Calvin and Zwingli the Reformed Church. But in England the Reformation resulted in the Anglican Church, the Presbyterian Church, the Independents or Congregationalists, and the Baptists. Further, it didn't entirely rout out Roman Catholicism. It took about a century and a half for all of these groups to learn to live together through the Act of Toleration in 1689. In fact, especially in the case of Ireland, now, even centuries later, tremendous difficulties are faced in trying to bring adherents of these different churches together in peace.

The British Reformers produced many texts that have had a lasting impact on the church, including The Thirty-Nine Articles, *The Book of Common Prayer*, *Foxe's Book of Martyrs*, and Knox's *Book of Discipline*. These figures and their books brought about lasting change in the church and in the spiritual life of the British. For some these theological reforms were satisfactory; for others, especially for the Puritans, they were not. In the next chapter we'll see how the Puritans took the Reformation that was started by a king seeking a divorce (or annulment to be more historically accurate) even further.

chapter seven

MEN IN BLACK

The Puritans and the British Reformation

Blessed are the pure in heart, for they shall see God.

MATTHEW 5:8

Few groups have been treated worse by historical memory than the Puritans. Even the word *puritanical* is an insult directed to a prudish, if not hypocritical, person. In a British context, the Puritans were seen as the ones who closed down the theaters—and this fresh on the heels of Shakespeare—instituted curfews, regulated dress, and demanded church attendance. The Puritans haven't fared much better in American contexts either. Most Americans have come to know everything they know about the Puritans through three literary vehicles: Nathaniel Hawthorne's *The Scarlet Letter* (1850); Arthur Miller's play *The Crucible* (1953), retelling the Salem witch trials in the frenzy of McCarthyism; and Jonathan Edwards's consummate Puritan sermon and high-school American literature survey text, "Sinners in the Hands of an Angry God."

The Puritans were fine purveyors of hypocrisy, rigidity, misogyny, and patriarchal-dominated hierarchy, not to mention gloom and doom, hellfire and brimstone. They were downright mean-spirited holier-than-thous. Or so the caricature goes. But Hawthorne's book and Miller's play are as close to the real thing as a picture in a magazine of a Hawaiian vacation is to a few weeks in the islands themselves. There are some vague connections between the picture and the vacation itself, but the real thing far outstrips any picture. So it is also with Edwards's sermon. He, along with the other Puritans, never shrank from preaching on hell

99

and the realities of judgment, of exclaiming God's wrath on sin and sinners. The famous "Sinners" sermon, however, is literally one straw of a whole heap of writings that he left behind. His lexicon overflows with the words *beauty* and *harmony*, *joy* and *pleasure*, *delight* and *love*. He could talk about sin and sorrow with the best of them, but he could also top just about anyone when it comes to grace and joy. We need, in other words, to get beyond the caricatures of the Puritans or we will never appreciate them for who they were and will never appreciate their rich legacy for us today.[1]

WHO ARE THE PURITANS?

The term *Puritan* was first a term of derision, devised by their opponents. Those who bore the label *Puritan* sought a pure church and a pure life, going against the grain of the moral and religious status quo. They took holiness seriously, both for the individual and for the redeemed community of the church. They were also called Non-conformists, which reveals a crucial piece of their identity. They refused to conform to the state church, to Anglicanism. This further earned them the title of Dissenters or Separatists, dissenting and separating from the national church. In reality, there were both Separatist and Non-Separatist Puritans. The Separatists viewed the Anglican Church as apostate, advocating utter separation from it. The Non-Separatists, while affirming that the true church is comprised of true saints, avoided taking such a hard line against the Anglicans. In fact, some Anglicans, even some bishops, were quite Puritan in their theology and outlook.

THE ACT AGAINST THE PURITANS, 1593

After passing another Act of Supremacy in 1559, reestablishing Anglicanism as the official church in England after Mary's reign, and after passing a number of Acts of Uniformity to further underscore Anglicanism as the only legal religion, Elizabeth passed the culminating Act Against the Puritans in 1593. It carried a stiff penalty for those who would not attend Anglican services or partake of Communion in Anglican churches, instead opting for the "disordered and unlawful conventicles and assemblies" of the Puritans. Those who were "lawfully convicted":

> Shall be committed to prison, there to remain without bail or mainprise, until they shall conform and yield themselves to come to such church, chapel, or usual place of common prayer, and hear divine service, according to her majesty's laws and statutes aforesaid [Acts of Supremacy and Uniformity], and to make such open submission and declaration of their said conformity, as hereafter in this Act is declared and appointed.

The Puritans' roots extend to the early days of the Reformation in England, as we saw in Chapter Six, and to the other Reformation movements. The date of their true birth, however, came about during the reign of Elizabeth I and her passing of the Law of Conformity in 1559, privileging the Anglican Church. The Puritans lasted until the 1660s, giving them a full century of life—in England, that is. In America they lasted a bit longer, stretching into the early decades of the eighteenth century. There were many of them, and they certainly liked to write (and write and write). Consequently, we have a rather eventful one hundred years and an immense literary legacy to consider.

The reforms in Britain, stemming from Henry VIII, Edward VI, and Elizabeth I, did not go far or deep enough for the Puritans. They were after something more, a truly theological reformation. Elizabeth I was followed by King James I, of the Bible version's fame. He didn't think much of the Puritans, exclaiming, "I shall make them conform themselves or I shall harry them out of the land." Since conforming wasn't an option, a group of Puritans in Scooby set sail for a place where they could have more religious liberties. They first stayed in the Netherlands, then embarked again to the New World where they could have freedom. They arrived at Plymouth Rock in what would become the colony and then the state of Massachusetts. Their charter gave them land in the "Northern parts" of Virginia—geography was much simpler before the fifty states.

PURITANS IN THE NEW WORLD

During the reigns of James I and Charles I, Puritans found it increasingly difficult to remain in England. Many fled for the Netherlands, resulting in rather large English-speaking congregations there. Others braved the wide sea to travel to the New World. Puritans reached the shores in waves from the first major settlements in 1620, traveling on the *Mayflower* and landing at Plymouth Rock, and in 1630, led by John Winthrop and establishing the Massachusetts Bay Colony. The 1620 group is technically the Pilgrims. Thomas Hooker (1586–1647) led a group from Massachusetts to found the colony of Connecticut in 1639. The Puritans dominated New England life and culture through the seventeenth century. By the early decades of the 1700s, their influence was waning, due to shifting cultural values and the aftermath of the Salem witch trials (1690s). Significant New England Puritans include the father and son team of Increase Mather (1639–1723) and Cotton Mather (1663–1728), John Cotton (1585–1652), Anne Bradstreet (1612–1672), and Jonathan Edwards (1703–1758)—often dubbed the last Puritan.

William Laud

For those Puritans who remained, things went from tolerable to worse under Charles I, who came to the throne in 1625 following James I's death. The real nightmare for the Puritans was Charles's ecclesiastical henchman, Archbishop William Laud. Charles I was, by just about all accounts, an inept ruler. A case in point was the upward trajectory of Laud. Laud was unpopular with his subordinates and colleagues, and yet at every opportunity Charles moved him up the ranks to the top seat in the Anglican Church. Laud saw to it that the laws on the books against the Non-Conformists were more than words on paper. He wanted them enforced, and he had a few new laws added as well. Once again Puritans left for the Netherlands or set sail for the New World, John Winthrop leading a group in 1630. The Puritans who stayed behind were ousted from their pulpits and from their positions in England's universities.

Laud's hard and fast reign over the church came to an end in the 1640s. Charles I's ineptitude caught up with him, plunging the nation into civil war. Parliament took on more power, and by 1641 boatloads of Puritan exiles crossed the North Sea and returned to England from the Netherlands. During the 1640s Parliament commissioned a rather large group of theologians to write creedal documents reflecting Reformed and Puritan theology and church polity or government. Meeting mostly in the Jerusalem Chamber of Westminster Abbey, this group of British and Scottish theologians and pastors eventually produced the Westminster Standards, the doctrinal statements for a number of denominations to this day.

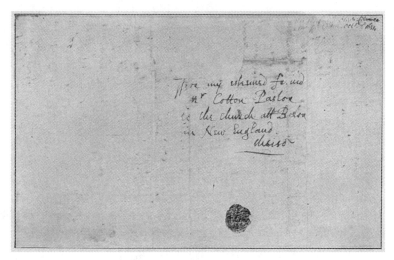

Letter from Oliver Cromwell to John Cotton

If the 1640s were a good time to be a Puritan, then the 1650s were even better, especially for the Independents and the Baptists. The Parliamentary forces were finally able to rout Charles I and his army, leaving Oliver Cromwell to be named Lord Protectorate, the first time in centuries that England was not ruled by a monarch. Cromwell was a Puritan through and through. Under him and the Puritan-controlled Parliament, laws reflecting Puritan beliefs and values were enacted, and Puritan ministers could preach freely. But then Cromwell died. After a failed attempt to put his son in the position of Lord Protectorate—even a number of Puritans, especially the Presbyterians, were concerned that this was going the way of another monarchy-by-birthright route—Charles II came to the throne, bringing his program of Restoration along with him.

Historians refer to Charles II's time as the Restoration because during it the monarchy and Parliament were restored to their rightful place (from the monarchy's perspective, of course) and the Church of England was restored to its rightful place, supplanting Puritanism's brief reign. The theaters were reopened, and civil life returned to its pre-Puritan days. Another law of conformity was passed, leaving many Puritans to once again flee their beloved England or find themselves in jail.

One such Puritan was John Bunyan. He was arrested for holding an illegal religious meeting and was originally sentenced to three months in jail. Since he refused to stipulate that he would not preach again upon release, his three-month sentence turned into twelve very long years. He figured out a way to pass the time, however—making a flute out of a four-legged stool—three legs work just as fine—and writing. He wrote many books in his lifetime, but none more famous than his allegory about a man who dreamed about a man with a burden on his back and a book in his hand. Bunyan called his main character Christian, and he titled his book *Pilgrim's Progress*. It is a classic of Puritan literature.[2]

When Charles II died, he was followed briefly by James II, who was Roman Catholic. This just wouldn't do since it had been more than a century since a Catholic was on the throne.[3] James II was rather peacefully sent into exile, and he was followed by the reign of William and Mary. The powers of the monarchy were greatly limited at this time, which historians refer to as the "bloodless revolution." The previous conformity laws were overturned, granting religious freedom. This was sealed in 1689 with the Act of Toleration. Puritanism was legislated both into and out of existence.

THE ACT OF TOLERATION, 1689

This Act begins by listing and then repealing the various Acts of Elizabeth I, James I, and Charles I that made dissent from the Anglican Church illegal. It is a long list. The Act proceeds to grant toleration for those Protestants who "scruple" over different church practices and beliefs. The Puritans still needed to register with the Anglican bishops and the justices of peace in their area, but they were free to meet and to preach. The penalty for not following this Act was not jail. A mere fine of a "sum of six pence" would do.

TASTING THE GOOD LIFE:
PURITAN BELIEFS AND PRACTICES

During their hundred years, the Puritans engaged in one primary activity—preaching. All of the Reformers agreed that the marks of the true church could be boiled down to one: the preaching of the Word. Luther said time and time again, "We can spare everything, except the Word." Unlike the great cathedrals with the pulpit to the side and the altar at the center, the Puritans put the pulpit in the middle, high and lifted up—as much for acoustics as for emphasis. The church, they believed, is about the preaching of the gospel. They had Paul's exhortation to Timothy ringing in their ears: Above all, preach the Word, preach the Word, preach the Word (2 Tim. 4:2).

As preachers, they not only preached a great deal (and long sermons at that), they also wrote. There are not too many modern-day counterparts to John Owen's magisterial eight- or four-volume, depending on how it gets packaged, commentary on Hebrews. These volumes were first preached as sermons. But lest we think of the Puritans as preachers and hearers of the Word only, they also were doers of the Word. Puritanism was a lived religion that permeated every area of life, every relationship, and every activity. Puritans endeavored to preach and live the Word of God by the grace of God for the glory of God. For them this was the good life.

If you were living in England and you wanted to be a Puritan, you would have done no better than to enroll at Emmanuel College, Cambridge University. This was the hotbed of Puritanism. For proof, just about all of the original male founders of New England were Emmanuel alumni. As a student there, your first assignment would be to memorize William Ames's *The Marrow of Theology*, in its original Latin of course.[4]

From the very first page we can see what the Puritans were up to. Ames says theology is "the doctrine or teaching of living to God." To put it more succinctly, theology is the Godward life. Studying the art of living, he further tells us, is our most noble pursuit, and since living for God is the highest form of living, studying the Godward life is the noblest of all pursuits. He declares, "Theology is better defined as that good life whereby we live to God." These days a number of advertisements touting the good life sell everything from furniture to cars. Ames tells us that the real thing is theology, the good life is the Godward life, and the Godward life is the theological life. It is a life of knowing God, seeing God, walking with God. The Puritans not only told us that we should live theologically—they also showed us how to do it. A convenient frame for living theologically, and for getting at the heart of Puritan beliefs, is found in the last few phrases of the Apostles' Creed.

" I believe in . . . the holy catholic [universal] church, the communion of saints." Puritanism was forged in the context of Roman Catholicism and of burgeoning Anglicanism. Being a member of the church was a matter of one's birth, one's national identity. Prior to 1534, anyone who was a citizen of the Holy Roman Empire living in England and had been baptized as an infant was automatically a member of the Roman Catholic Church. After 1534 the same qualifications fit one for membership in the Anglican Church. The Puritans couldn't go along with that. While most of them held to infant baptism, there were Puritans who held to believer's baptism. But all of the Puritans, infant and believer's baptism adherents alike, firmly believed that one must "own the covenant."

This last phrase, used so often by the Puritans, means that one becomes a member of the true church by confessing the work of Christ on the cross and clinging to the merits of his righteousness. The Puritans spoke of "visible sainthood," referring to the idea that the church is to be made up of true saints who profess Christ and seek to live for him. The Puritans believed wholeheartedly in the holy, catholic (universal) church, and only those who believe in Christ can be members of this church. Being taken to the baptismal font as an infant is no guarantee of entrance into the church. This marked the Puritans off from Roman Catholics and Anglicans.

Then there's the phrase "the communion of the saints." Again this stresses the distinctly Puritan view of the church. Church is not a social club but a group of people brought together by a truly common union in Jesus Christ and in one's common standing at the foot of the cross. The

Puritan understanding of the church as a communion of saints led them to take church discipline seriously. But there's also a positive side. The Puritans suffered persecution, sometimes finding themselves in jail and more often than not finding themselves on the margins of society. During these tough times they savored the communion of saints. They found courage in corporate worship, comfort in the Lord's Supper, and solace in the preaching of the Word of God. It was Bunyan, while in prison, who wrote of the church as "the house built by the Lord of the Hill . . . for the relief and security of pilgrims" in *Pilgrim's Progress*. The Puritans knew by firsthand experience the sweetness of these words.

"I believe in . . . the forgiveness of sins." The Puritans understood what it means to be holy and to be a saint because they understood sin. In fact, they could only understand holiness because they understood sin. They didn't fixate on sin due to some psychological hang-up, despite what Hawthorne might have thought. They weren't prudes and killjoys. They did know, however, the condition of their hearts. Hawthorne invites us to mock sin and the concepts of guilt and shame that come with it as he unfolds the tumult in the life of Hester Prynne, his novel's heroine. Against Hawthorne, the Puritans remind us that sin and its attendant guilt and shame are all too real. They didn't invent sin or guilt or shame as mere cultural conventions to keep control of the group. They knew the power of sin, guilt, and shame to wreak havoc in their own lives and in the lives of those they loved.

NOTABLE PURITANS AND THEIR BOOKS

The Puritans are often referred to as "people of the Book," revealing the centrality of the Bible to them. They were also people of books, revealing the plethora of books they wrote and loved to read. This list captures a mere handful of Puritan books currently available.[5]

Puritan Books on Preaching and the Pastoral Ministry
William Perkins (1558–1602), *The Art of Prophesying [Preaching]* (1592)
Richard Baxter (1615–1691), *The Reformed Pastor* (1656)

Puritan Books on Theology
William Ames (1576–1633), *The Marrow of Theology* (1642)
Thomas Watson (?–1686), *A Body of Divinity* (1692)

Puritan Books on the Christian Life
Richard Sibbes (1577–1635), *The Bruised Reed* (1630)
Jeremiah Burroughs (1599–1646), *The Rare Jewel of Christian Contentment* (1648)
John Owen (1616–1683), *Communion with God* (1657)
Jonathan Edwards (1703–1758), *Religious Affections* (1746)

They didn't merely believe in sin, however. They believed in the *forgiveness of* sin. Guilt is real, but so is grace. Read anywhere in the Puritan writings, and you will bump into the ugliness of sin. Keep reading, and you will see the beauty of grace and the power of God in his mercy to wipe sinful hearts clean through the merits of Christ. They knew sin to be powerful, but they knew the gospel to be more so. They knew the damage sin brings, and they knew the restoration that grace brings. They knew that humanity lost a great deal in the Fall, but they also knew, along with Paul, that humanity gained much more through Christ in redemption. For more, read John Owen's *On the Mortification of Sin* or the great epic poems of John Milton, *Paradise Lost* and *Paradise Regained*. Milton captures the Puritan view of sin and redemption well in the opening lines of *Paradise Lost*:

> *Of man's first disobedience, and the fruit*
> *Of that forbidden tree whose mortal taste*
> *Brought death into the World, and all our woe,*
> *With loss of Eden, till one greater Man*
> *Restore us, and regain that blissful seat.*

"I believe in . . . the resurrection of the body, and life everlasting." The Puritans realized that this life is not all there is. They acknowledged their frailty and longed for the day when they would have their resurrected bodies. There is a resurrection. There is eternity. This belief led them to view this life as the pilgrim life, as a journey from this world to the next, from the City of Destruction to the Celestial City, to use Bunyan's words. This longing for the world to come was far from escapism for the Puritans. Contrary to public opinion, they enjoyed life and lived fully. As J. I. Packer and Leland Ryken, among others, have shown, they engaged the arts and not only longed for heaven but sought to make this world a better place as they traveled through it.[6] This is mainly due to the fact that as they lived their lives, they were filled with hope. The hope of sins forgiven. The hope of the life to come. The hope of enjoying God unclogged by sin. Among the many Puritans who so well illustrate this, Jeremiah Burroughs stands as a good example.

A RARE JEWEL: THE EXAMPLE OF JEREMIAH BURROUGHS

Jeremiah Burroughs, born in 1599, was trained at Emmanuel College, receiving his B.A. and M.A. He began his ministry in the region of East Anglia, England, a Puritan stronghold. He sided with the Independents. Puritanism is a bit of an umbrella term, encompassing some Anglicans, Presbyterians, Independents or Congregationalists (this is the group that landed in New England), and Baptists. They all held to the *Solas* of the Reformation, Calvinism, and Reformed theology, but they differed over views of church government and over baptism, in the case of the Baptists. But Burroughs wore his Congregationalism lightly. When he died, it was said of him by Richard Baxter, "If all the Episcopalians had been like Archbishop Ussher, all the Presbyterians like Stephen Marshall, and all the Independents like Jeremiah Burroughs, then the breaches of the church would soon have been healed."

Burroughs was getting along well in his ministry when the bishop in that region, Matthew Wren (the uncle of Britain's famous architect Christopher Wren), turned up the heat on the Puritans, demanding among other things that ministers read the Book of Sports from the pulpit on Sunday. The Book of Sports (1618) was King James I's attempt at a national physical fitness program, only with a distinct twist. When James was traveling one Sunday, he noticed a number of towns where the youth were just lulling around when they could have been engaged in the rigors of sport. When he inquired of his attendants why the boys weren't on the athletic fields on such a fine day, they informed him that they were in Puritan territory. The Puritans, of course, frowned on such activity on the Sabbath. James responded by publishing the Book of Sports.

IMPORTANT EVENTS FOR PURITANISM

1534—Act of Supremacy (Henry VIII): England declares its ecclesiastical independence from Rome

1553–1558—Reign of Bloody Mary: a time of religious persecution in England

1559–1564—Acts of Uniformity and Conformity (Elizabeth I): Puritanism is legislated into existence

1620s—Reign of Charles I and Archbishop William Laud: a time of religious persecution of the Puritans; many flee for the Netherlands and the New World

1640s—England's Civil War: King versus Parliament; Westminster Assembly meets

1650s—Cromwell's reign: a time of Puritan ascendancy in England

1662—Act of Uniformity (Charles II): restoration of Anglicanism; time of persecution of Puritans

1664—Conventicle Act: bans Puritan preaching and church services

1689—Act of Toleration (William and Mary): Puritanism is legislated out of existence

During Charles I's reign, Archbishop Laud saw the Book of Sports as a convenient tool to irritate the Puritans. He had Charles I not only push the Book of Sports but require that ministers read it from the pulpit to inspire the youth and their parents to get out and get active on the Sabbath afternoon. It worked, sharply irritating Puritan ministers. Some of them consented. They would read from the Book of Sports only to add immediately upon finishing the reading the command from Exodus 20:8. They would say, having finished reading the Book of Sports, "Hear then the word of the king. Now, hear the word of our Lord, 'Remember the Sabbath day, to keep it holy.'" Other ministers just couldn't bring themselves to read it in the pulpit. So they stepped down and went into exile. Jeremiah Burroughs was among this latter group. He set sail for Rotterdam. While there, he served as pastor in an English-speaking church that had been founded by William Ames.

Burroughs's exile only lasted from 1637–1641. Upon his return, he was invited to address Parliament, making quite the triumphal reentry. Here is what he said on that occasion:

Now we are come and find peace and mercy here, the voice of joy and gladness. We scarce thought that we should ever see our country again, but behold we are here with our honorable senators and worthies of our land and called by them to rejoice with them, and to praise our God in the great congregation.

From 1641 until his death in 1646, Burroughs was active in the work of the Westminster Assembly. He also pastored two congregations, one at St Giles Cripplegate, where John Milton lies buried in the churchyard, and one at Stepney in Northeast London. In October 1646, after being thrown from a horse, Burroughs contracted a fever and died on November 13, 1646. Soon after his death, his books came off the printing press. Owing to the Puritan sense of humility and modesty, it was common for the Puritans to have their books published after they died rather than while they lived. Burroughs's posthumously published works include commentaries on Hosea and the Beatitudes, various books on the Christian life, and his classic work, *The Rare Jewel of Christian Contentment*, published in 1648. This book grew out of the need to learn the lesson of contentment during a season of want and suffering. Contentment, however, is also a lesson to be learned during times of abundance and prosperity. In fact, ironically, times of abundance can be the winter of discontent.

London, 1647

Burroughs defines contentment early on in his book, observing, "Christian Contentment is that sweet, inward, quiet, gracious frame of spirit, which freely submits to and delights in God's wise and fatherly disposal in every condition." Contentment is not a rare jewel because it is a secret or some hidden knowledge. It's a rare jewel because it is so hard to live out in one's life. It's an "art," as Burroughs calls it, learned by practice and acquired skill. It's hard because our natural tendency is toward "murmuring" or complaining. Among his many pointers for living a life of contentment against the grain of culture and human nature, Burroughs reminds us of the promises of God that are ours. "The saints of God," he assures us, "have an interest in all the promises that ever were made to our forefathers . . . all the promises made in all the book of God." While this doesn't always solve all immediate problems and trials, it does offer a healthy perspective.[7]

Burroughs also reminds us of our future hope, but he does so in a way that forces us to see that hope as a present reality. He notes that the Christian can have "contentment by realizing the glorious things of heaven to him. He has the kingdom of Heaven as present, and the glory that is to come; by faith he makes it present." Burroughs is but one of a whole cast of Puritans who have left a rich literary legacy for the church.

CONCLUSION

Thomas Macauley, England's great historian from the nineteenth century, famously put it like this: "The Puritans hated bear-baiting"—a popular sport somewhat akin to cockfights—"not because it gave pain to the bear, but because it gave pleasure to the spectators." Not to be outdone by Macauley is the remark of America's own curmudgeonly newspaperman and wordsmith H. L. Mencken, who said, "Puritanism is the haunting fear that someone, somewhere might just be having a good time." Hopefully by now we have seen that such remarks on the Puritans could not be further from the truth. If you want prudishness, look to the Victorians. If you want a model for a full-throttled life of glorifying and enjoying God, look to the Puritans.

There were many outstanding Puritan scholars and theologians, such as John Owen, William Ames, and William Perkins. There were many outstanding pastors such as Jeremiah Burroughs, Richard Sibbes, and Thomas Goodwin. There were outstanding writers and poets, such as John Milton, John Bunyan, and Anne Bradstreet.[8] They were Anglicans, Presbyterians, Independents or Congregationalists, and Baptists. Some were imprisoned, some exiled, some martyred. Some enjoyed places of position in British society. They dominated all of life in New England for its first full century. They are more often misunderstood and overlooked than appreciated and taken seriously. They can be intimidating, even to their would-be friends. Nevertheless, they have left a significant legacy for the church.

Their unique contribution to the Reformation may be summed up by the estimates of two historians. First, A. G. Dickens notes that the Puritans weren't looking for a national church but essentially formed a "religious club for athletes," which is to say they took the church very seriously. More recently, Patrick Collinson has paid them the supreme compliment by noting, "It is hardly an exaggeration to say that [Puritanism] was the real English Reformation."[9] They weren't looking for a national church, and they weren't interested in minor adjustments to the status quo. The Puritans knew that the church needed deep and wide reforms, and that's exactly what they sought to do.

chapter eight

WOMEN IN BLACK TOO

The Untold Story of Women and the Reformation

The home, cities, economic life, and government would virtually disappear. Men can't do without women. Even if it were possible for men to beget and bear children, they still couldn't do without women.

MARTIN LUTHER

Martin Luther, Ulrich Zwingli, John Calvin, Conrad Grebel, Menno Simons, Thomas Cranmer, John Bunyan, Jeremiah Burroughs—all of them have at least one thing in common. They're all men. When the story of the Reformation gets told, it's typically their story. There is another story to be told, however—the inspiring story of the courage and fortitude of the women of the Reformation. Their too often untold story needs to be heard.

The women of the Reformation fit into two categories: Reformers' wives who made quite an impact themselves and women who made substantive contributions on their own. Among the first category, none is more well-known than Katherina von Bora, the former nun who married Martin Luther. In the latter category we find mostly nobility and even royalty—some risking great wealth and family honor for their commitment to the Reformation cause. All of them played significant roles.

The official dogma of the Roman Catholic Church disallowed a married clergy. Monks and the ranks of the clergy were married to the church; nuns were married to Christ. Breaking the vow of celibacy whether theoretically or officially would mean that one would have to give up a position in the church. Unofficially and practically, of course, there were secret marriages and mistresses and affairs. Thomas Cranmer, for instance, had a wife long before he and Henry VIII brought about the British Reformation. When Ulrich Zwingli became priest of the Great Minster at Zurich he was replacing a "celibate" priest who somehow managed to father a number of children.

The Reformers, with Luther and Calvin leading the way, championed the institution of marriage and the family. They saw no biblical warrant for the celibacy of the priesthood—Peter, after all, had a mother-in-law. Conversely, they saw marriage elevated and celebrated everywhere in the pages of Scripture. Once they got married, however, they faced a challenge that the church as a whole hadn't faced in over a millennium: What does a minister's family look like? Just as they broke new ground on so many areas of theology, they also needed to pioneer the Christian home. Fortunately, they were not alone. They had formidable wives to help them figure it out.

MARRIED TO THE REFORMATION

While Katherina von Bora might be the most famous of the Reformation wives, she didn't quite compare with Wibrandis Rosenblatt, at least not when it came to the number of husbands. She was Wibrandis (Rosenblatt) Keller-Oecolampadius-Capito-Bucer. Yes, she had four husbands, and all of them were significant Reformers, causing one writer to dub her "the Bride of the Reformation," or as she is known in German, the *Reformationfrau*.[1] Wibrandis and her widowed mother lived in Basel, where she met her first husband, Ludwig Keller. He died after just two short years of marriage, leaving Wibrandis widowed at the age of twenty-two and the mother of a small child, also named Wibrandis. She soon after married Johannes Oecolampadius (1482–1531)—his last name means "house lamp"—a leader in the Swiss Reformation. Having been a Roman Catholic priest, Oecolampadius gave up being a bachelor at the age of forty-five. After four years of marriage and having a son named Eusebius, after the famed historian of the early church, Wibrandis was again left a widow when Oecolampadius died on November 23, 1531. "Pray the Lord to give us a long and happy marriage," Oecolampadius had written to William Farel, his friend in Geneva. It wasn't to be.[2]

Johannes Oecolampadius

At about the same time that Oecolampadius died, his friend and fellow Reformer at Strasbourg, Wolfgang Capito (1478–1541), lost his wife. Martin Bucer, a friend and a frequent visitor in Oecolampadius's home, served as matchmaker for the widow and the widower. The next year Wibrandis packed her home and took her two children off to Strasbourg. Tragedy would soon strike, however, as the plague ravaged Strasbourg, taking the lives of Eusebius Oecolampadius, the two children of Wibrandis and Wolfgang Capito, and the life of Capito himself. The plague also claimed the life of Elisabeth Bucer, the wife of Martin. For a third time, Wibrandis was widowed.

KATHERINE ZELL (1498–1558)

At one point in her life Katherine Zell was called "Doctor Katrina," to which she could only reply, "I am not usurping the office of preacher or apostle. I am like the dear Mary Magdalene, who with no thought of being an apostle, came to tell the disciples that she had encountered the risen Lord." Katherine Schutz had converted from Catholicism upon reading a work by Martin Luther and listening to the sermons of Matthew Zell in her hometown of Strasbourg. Zell must have been some preacher, for within a few years, on December 3, 1523 (at 6 A.M.), they were married. Katherine Zell went on to write some pamphlets of her own, one of them defending their marriage. The Zells and Martin Bucer brought the

Reformation to Strasbourg. When Calvin was exiled there, he spent his first few weeks in the Zells' home.

The Zells knew their share of suffering. They lost two children in infancy, suffered the impugning of their character, and felt the sting of the Peasants' War in 1525. In one of her pamphlets offering comfort to other wives and women who were experiencing suffering, Katherine Zell wrote, "Faith is not faith which is not tried."[3]

In 1542 Wibrandis entered her fourth marriage to, of course, Martin Bucer (1491–1551). In 1548 the Reformation in Switzerland took a turn for the worse, causing the hard-line Reformers to look for freer environs. Bucer headed for Cambridge, England, where, under the reign of Edward VI, he had a great influence in preaching and teaching. The climate, food, and culture, however, never quite agreed with Bucer. He died in 1551. This was actually the longest marriage that Wibrandis had, even though it only lasted nine years. After Bucer's death, Wibrandis returned with the family to Strasbourg before returning to her first home of Basel. There were no children in the marriage to Bucer, but there were children from Bucer's first and children from her previous marriages. She lived until 1564, when the plague again swept through Basel. Wibrandis (Rosenblatt) Keller-Oecolampadius-Capito-Bucer was truly married to the Reformation and was a matriarch of the Swiss Reformation.

Wibrandis's marriages were punctuated by tragedy, yet she persevered. Children died in infancy. Her husbands faced uphill struggles as they fought for the Reformation. Finances were stretched thin. She cared for her widowed mother. Her home was more like a hostel, full of travelers and children and relatives. Bucer once said of her, "I can only hope to be as kind to my new wife as she to me." She could write in German and Latin, and according to her second husband, Oecolampadius, she knew her theology. But she was always in the shadows, her contribution never applauded, her role not to be center stage. Could Keller, Oecolampadius, Capito, and Bucer have done what they did without her?

John Calvin drew the same strength from his brief and tragedy-filled marriage to Idellete de Bure. They had one child, a son who died in infancy. After nine years of marriage, Idelette was brought low by illness. She never enjoyed good health throughout the course of their marriage. She died in 1549. Calvin was devastated. Writing to his friend and fellow Reformer Pierre Viret, he declared his grief: "I have been bereaved of the best companion of my life." To Farel he stated, "I do what I can to keep myself from being overwhelmed by grief." He recalled their last few moments together. "She was unable to speak, and her mind seemed to be troubled. I, having spoken a few words about the love of Christ, the hope of eternal life, concerning our married life, and her departure, engaged in prayer. In full possession of her mind, she both heard the prayer and attended to it."[4] Calvin could never find a companion of equal stature to Idelette, remaining a widower until his death in 1564.

And then there's Martin Luther's Katherina von Bora, or "Katie, my rib," as he called her. As we mentioned in Chapter Two, Luther thought himself to be a confirmed bachelor until Katie came along. Luther's literary output was incredible. He preached and taught and consulted and administered tirelessly. But he couldn't manage a household for anything. Those of more noble standing showered him with gifts of money and property. Most of it slipped through Luther's hands as quickly as it came into them. Luther just didn't seem to have room for thinking about such things. Katie managed it all expertly.

Luther was traveling when he fell ill and died. Just weeks after his death, Katie wrote to a sister-in-law, "Yes, my sorrow is so deep that no words can express my heartbreak. . . . I can neither eat nor drink, not even sleep. . . . God knows that when I think of having lost him, I can neither talk nor write in all my suffering and crying." She would sign her letters "solitary widow." The following years were not easy for her. She had her children to attend to, and after her famous husband's death, many simply forgot about the Luther family. As was said in her eulogy, "She experienced much ingratitude by many people of whom she should expect help and support for the sake of her husband's public merits in the service to the church." Her self-description near the end has her "clinging to Christ like a burr to a dress." She died in 1552.[5]

THE COURAGE OF QUEENS

One of the shortest reigns of any monarch perhaps of all time lasted only nine days. In some sense her reign was a front, she being a puppet with the strings controlled by her handlers, not the least of which was her father. Yet Lady Jane Grey (1537–1554), England's famed "Nine Day Queen," had a mind all her own. Jane Grey, as portrayed in a major motion picture, is seen in historical memory as precocious, if not irascible, depicted as a teenager bent on finding herself and asserting herself, right up to the end when she dies heroically. The movie errs most, however, in paying too slim attention to the theological and religious dimension of Jane Grey. Her handlers knew they were getting a Protestant, but they didn't know they were getting a Protestant theologian. Jane, barely in her teen years, corresponded regularly with Heinrich Bullinger, Zwingli's successor in Switzerland. One time she asked him about the best course of study for learning Hebrew.

LADY JANE GREY TO HER SISTER, CATHERINE

I have here sent you, good sister Catherine, a book, which although it be not outwardly trimmed with gold, yet inwardly it is worth more than precious stones. It is the book, dear sister, of the law of the Lord. . . .

Rejoice in Christ, as I do. Follow the steps of your master Christ, and take up your cross. Lay your sins on his back, and always embrace him. And as touching my death, rejoice as I do, good sister, that I shall be delivered of this corruption, and put on incorruption. For I am assured, that I shall, for losing of a mortal life, win an immortal life.

When Edward VI died, at a young age but not entirely unexpectedly, the court went into a tailspin. Mary, soon to be Bloody Mary, was the rightful heir, being the daughter of Henry VIII and Catherine of Aragon. She was Catholic to the core, and her ascent to the throne threatened to unravel the entire Reformation in Britain. Those committed to seeing the Reformation through entered into a backroom political blitz, resulting in the plan to put Jane Grey on the throne.

They plied her status as the great-niece of Henry VIII to qualify her for the throne (Jane Grey's mother was daughter to Henry VIII's sister—remember this for the quiz). Everyone, however, could see straight through the transparent plot to undermine England's long-held belief in the divine right of kings, which means in short, don't mess with the bloodline in the accession of the throne. Even though Mary was Catholic, not putting her on the throne would have been tantamount to reversing the course of the planets. In other words, Jane Grey enjoyed only a small circle of support because even many friends of the Reformation could not go against the divine right of the monarchy. Mary's forces easily routed the meager army defending Jane Grey. Those who put her on the throne and Jane Grey herself all ended up in the Tower of London. They were the first to fall in Mary's reign of terror and revenge, revenge both on the Protestant "heretics" for deposing Roman Catholicism and on those who co-conspired in the "annulment" of Henry VIII's marriage to Mary's mother, Catherine of Aragon. Those long decades Mary spent in exile in France provided ample opportunity for her to nurse both her Catholicism and her plans of vengeance.

After Mary had Jane Grey arrested in 1553, however, she attempted to show her mercy, pitying her as a pawn in the sordid plot, as she herself had been as a child. If Jane Grey would but take the Roman Mass, Mary would give Jane her life. Jane was sixteen years of age at this time, which meant that she had quite a bit of life to consider living. But the price proved too high. Jane Grey refused, adamant in her Protestant beliefs to the last. So adamant was she in her beliefs that she chastised her family's chaplain for conveniently converting to Catholicism when Mary came to power. "Wilt thou refuse the true God, and worship the invention of man, the golden calf, the whore of Babylon, the Romish religion, the abominable idol, the most wicked mass?" she wrote. Jane Grey took theology seriously. Imagine if she had a pulpit.[6]

After her arrest, Lady Jane was quizzed by Mary's archbishop, Feckenham, in the chapel at the Tower of London before an audience of Mary's supporters, which is to say before a Roman Catholic audience. Jane Grey withstood Feckenham's challenges of her rejection of the Roman view of the Lord's Supper, outfoxed him in arguing for the Reformation principle of *Sola Scriptura* (Scripture Alone), and got the upper hand on the issue of justification and our standing before God.

In the exchange over justification, Feckenham tried to trip her up by accusing her of rejecting good works, so clearly required of the Christian. "It is necessary unto salvation to do good works also; it is not sufficient only to believe," he told her. She returned, "I deny that, and I affirm that faith only saves; but it is meet for a Christian to do good works, in token that he follows the steps of his Master, Christ, yet may we not say that we profit to our salvation; for when we have done all, we are unprofitable servants, and faith only in Christ's blood saves us."[7] Luther could scarcely have put the doctrine of justification by faith better. On February 12, 1554, two days after her interview with Feckenham, Lady Jane Grey, the nine-day queen, was martyred for her beliefs. Her last words upon the scaffold were, "I here die a true Christian woman and I trust to be saved by the blood of Christ, and by none other means."[8]

At least Jane Grey has survived in memory. Jeanne D'Albret (1528–1572), Queen of Navarre, has essentially not, which is surely to our loss. Jeanne became ruler of Navarre, a small but crucial state interposed between Spain and France, after her father Henry died in 1555. By 1560 she publicly declared her allegiance to Protestantism and Calvinism. The territories under her control likewise became Protestant. She received a congratulatory letter from Calvin himself. "I cannot adequately express my joy," he wrote, and this from one who found a way to express himself on just about everything.[9] Not everyone received the news with equal fervor. The pope excommunicated her. The rulers in Spain thought that was justified because she took her lands by force. France, however, rather curiously supported her, not moving against her as the pope wished. That was surprising, of course, because of France's deeply embedded Catholicism.

Jeanne of Navarre's reign occasioned the display of her prowess at theology. She came by it honestly, learning from the example of her mother, Marguerite de Navarre, a frequent correspondent of Calvin and a significant force in the Reformation in France. Marguerite, though officially remaining Catholic to the end, embraced both the Reformers and Reformation principles. Sympathetic to Luther and to the Swiss Reformers, she read their Latin and German works, even translating some of Luther's writings into French. She wrote marvelously about devotion to God. She, at her own risk, defended persecuted Protestants in France.

Roland Bainton wrote of Marguerite that "she had so harrowed the soil of Navarre that it became the most fruitful field of the Huguenot movement to be spearheaded by her daughter, Jeanne d'Albret."[10]

MARIE DENTIERE, 1539

Marie Dentiere had been an abbotess before converting to the Reformation. She was trained in Geneva by Farel in the 1520s. She wrote two books, one a history of Geneva from 1526–1536. In addition she wrote many letters. This excerpt comes from a letter she wrote to Queen Marguerite of Navarre in April 1539.

I ask, didn't Jesus die just as much for the poor illiterates and the idiots as for the shaven, tonsured and mitred lords? Did he only say, "Go, preach my Gospel to the wise lords and grand doctors?" Did he not say, "To all?" Do we have two Gospels, one for men and the other for women? One for the educated and the other for the multitude? Are we not all one in our savior?

Cited in Katharina M. Wilson, ed., *Women Writers of the Renaissance and Reformation* (Athens, GA: The University of Georgia Press, 1987), page 260.

During the reign of Queen Jeanne, the lands of Navarre and Bearn became a further stronghold for the Huguenots, and they indeed prospered. Queen Jeanne, however, foresaw the need to provide for the future of Protestants in France. She went to the King of France's court to arrange a marriage for her son that would secure his ascension to the throne in France. She also had a plan to secure a permanent region in France that would be a safe haven for Protestants. The marriage was granted, but not the permanent Protestant region. She died of tuberculosis in 1572, just two months prior to her son's wedding. The wedding actually proved disastrous for France's Protestant future, which all but came crashing down in August 1572.

Many of the Huguenot leaders gathered in Paris for the wedding, held on August 18. Catherine de Medici, the Queen of France who at first tolerated the Huguenots and the wedding, seized the opportunity to purge France of its Protestant stain. And with Queen Jeanne dead, nothing stood in Catherine's way. On August 23, St. Bartholomew's Day, the slaughter began. In Paris alone over two thousand were martyred. By the time it ran its course, the St. Bartholomew's Day Massacre, as it came to be known, claimed over twenty thousand Huguenots throughout France.[11] It takes its place in history as one of the bloodiest episodes in the tumultuous history of the Reformation.

Jeanne's son, Henry, kept his life by taking the Roman Mass. He would eventually become the King of France, being dubbed Henry IV. As king, he embraced Catholicism in order to bring peace. "Paris is worth a Mass," he famously quipped. Had his mother lived to hear that, she would have been devastated.

THE HUGUENOTS AND THE FRENCH REFORMATION

The word *Huguenot* derives from the German word *eidgenossen*, meaning "confederated," and refers to the Swiss Protestants who were confederated against the Papal Swiss cities. The term has come to be used broadly to refer to Protestants in France during the time of the Reformation to the present day. Huguenots presently number seven hundred thousand. The Protestant Reformation never fared as well in France as it had elsewhere. The seasons of religious freedom were few and short-lived for those committed to Reformation theology. Most of the time they were persecuted and forced underground. Many Huguenots fled to Geneva, were trained by Calvin and others, and then returned to found churches and evangelize. The Edict of Nantes (1598) by France's King Henry IV brought about a time of freedom for the Huguenots. The edict was repealed in 1610. An intense time of persecution, led by Cardinal Richelieu, followed.

Jeanne d'Albret of Navarre's dreams for a Protestant France would not be realized. France would officially be Roman Catholic, the surviving Huguenots forced underground. Without the assistance of the mother and daughter Marguerite and Jeanne of Navarre, however, the Huguenots would have been in even more dire straits. Jeanne had once written that there is no greater obligation for a monarch "whom [God] has saved from sin and death by his grace and goodness alone" than "to procure the complete establishment and advancement of [Christ's] kingdom."[12]

THE PIETY OF POETS

Though she wasn't born on American soil, Anne Bradstreet takes her place as America's first poet. She was born in 1612 in England. By 1619 her father, Thomas Dudley, served as steward for the Earl of Lincoln, granting his daughter access to the world of learning contained in the earl's library, and she likely shared in the tutelage received by the earl's children. She learned theology through the Geneva Bible and reading Puritan works, then fresh off the printer's press. While at the Earl of Lincoln's estate, she met Simon Bradstreet, who had been the earl's charge since he was orphaned at the age of fourteen. They married in 1628, he at the age of twenty-five and she having just turned sixteen. As Charles I and his infamous archbishop Laud turned up the heat on the Puritans, the Bradstreets and Dudleys set off for the safe haven of the New World in 1630. They arrived at the harbor of Salem, Massachusetts, after two long months at sea.

Anne Bradstreet

Both Anne's father and husband would take the role of governor of the Massachusetts Bay Colony. She would, like every other colonial woman, carve out a life in the so often referred to "howling wilderness" of early New England. Unlike other colonial women, and men for that matter, she would also write poetry. John Woodbridge, Anne Bradstreet's brother-in-law, took her poetry back across the sea to old England, resulting in the 1650 publication of *The Tenth Muse Lately Sprung up in America*. Bradstreet did not know of Woodbridge's plans, and no one was as shocked as she to see the book.

Her work is poetic theology, evincing the influence of both poets and Puritan theologians. She gave perhaps the finest expression of the Puritan emphasis of the "pilgrim" life of the Christian, rivaled only by Bunyan's *Pilgrim's Progress*. This theme reverberates throughout her work, reaching a crescendo in her poem, "As Weary Pilgrim, Now at Rest." In the middle of the poem she sighs:

> *A Pilgrim I, on earth, perplext,*
> *wth sinnes wth cares and sorrows vext*
> *By age and paines brought to decay*
> *And my clay house mouldring away*
> *Oh how I long to be at rest*
> *and soar on high among the blest.*[13]

In a lengthy letter to her children recalling her own life's pilgrimage, she writes of times "in sicknesse, weaknes, paines," of times when she and her children suffered. Of these times, she further declares, "I have found them the Times when the Lord hath manifested the most Love to me."[14] She could further testify of God:

> *My hungry Soul he filled with Good,*
> *He in his Bottle putt my tears,*
> *My smarting wounds washt in his blood,*
> *And banisht thence my Doubts and feares.*[15]

Bradstreet once wrote of scoffers of her poetry who thought a knitting needle fit her hands better than a quill. The German poet Anna Owena Hoyers (1584–1655) faced a similar challenge. She also presents her detractors poetically:

> *Who say: it is not right*
> *That a woman should write.*

Hoyers has been described as a "profoundly Christian" Renaissance poet, which is to say that she did not share in the narrow humanism of other Renaissance figures. God and Christ figure prominently in her poetry.[16]

Marguerite of Navarre, mentioned above, also wrote poetry. Her tribute to Luther is seen in her poem on the Reformation doctrine of justification by faith alone. She writes:

> *To you I testify*
> *That God does justify*
> *Through Christ, the man who sins.*
> *But if he does not believe*
> *And by faith receive*
> *He shall have no peace,*
> *From worry no cease,*
> *God will then relieve,*
> *If faith will but believe*
> *Through Christ, the gentle Lord.*[17]

When Anna Hoyers rhetorically posed the question, "Who say: it is not right/That a woman should write," she was making a significant point. When Anne Bradstreet took up a quill, she was doing the church a service, for which we should be grateful. In persecution and in poetry, the women of the Reformation can and should be seen and heard.

CONCLUSION

Reformation scholars are divided on the issue of what the Reformation in fact accomplished for women. Steven Ozment has led the way for the view that the elevation of women and marriage and families is nearly the singular achievement of the Reformation's impact on culture. Others, such as Lyndal Roper, argue that the Reformation did little by way of the female gender. If judged by certain standards, the Reformation may in fact be seen as making little headway for women. At least in Roman Catholicism women had the capacity to serve the church officially in the convent. The Protestant Reformers, who restricted ordination to men, had very little to offer in a similar vein. Further, the Reformers believed in male headship in the home, and some, like John Knox, had serious problems with women in positions of civic leadership—though, in fairness to Knox, he objected more to Mary and Elizabeth's religious views than he did to their gender.[18]

Yet Ozment should not be so readily dismissed in his estimation. The Reformation indeed brought a new dignity to women and to marriage. He argues compellingly that the patriarchal households provided a refuge for women at a time and place in history when women had little if any rights. It was, after all, Calvin's Geneva that enacted laws against wife abuse and enacted more equitable laws of inheritance for widows and daughters. Ozment is persuasive when he tells us it's an injustice to the Reformers to underplay their achievements for women.

The Reformation is not only about the achievements *for* women, however. It also chronicles the achievements *of* women. Lady Jane Grey, Marguerite and Jeanne of Navarre, Anne Bradstreet, and others have a legacy all their own, each making significant contributions to the Reformation and the founding of Protestantism. Yet their stories have too often gone untold. The church of today can only benefit by telling and retelling them again.

Appendix

IN THEIR OWN WORDS:
SELECTIONS FROM
DOCUMENTS OF
THE REFORMATION

TEXTS OF
THE REFORMATION

The author of Ecclesiastes famously referred to the never-ending making of books. What's remarkable about the statement is that he made it long before the printing press and the explosion of books in the Reformation era. If the Reformation was about anything, it was about books, all centered around *the* Book, the Bible. Readings from the three texts below are a mere fraction of the flood of literature produced during the Reformation.

THE NINETY-FIVE THESES

This is the document that started it all. Luther, the monk with mallet in hand, nailed this document to the church door in Wittenberg on October 31, 1517, seeking a debate with the Roman Church. The selection here is reprinted from Stephen J. Nichols, editor, *Martin Luther's Ninety-Five Theses* (Phillipsburg, NJ: P&R, 2002).

1. When our Lord and Master Jesus Christ said "Repent," he intended that the entire life of believers should be repentance.

2. This word *repentance* cannot be understood to mean the sacrament of penance, or the act of confession and satisfaction administered by the priests.

21. Therefore, those preachers of indulgences are in error, who say that by the pope's indulgences a man is freed from every penalty and is saved.

24. Therefore, the greater part of the people are necessarily deceived by that indiscriminate and high-sounding promise of release from penalty.

27. They preach man-made doctrines who say that as soon as the coin jingles in the money-box, the soul flies out of purgatory.

50. Christians are to be taught that if the pope knew the exactions of the indulgence preachers, he would rather that St. Peter's church should go to ashes than that it should be built up with the skin, flesh, and bones of his sheep.

53. They are enemies of Christ and the pope who bid the word of God to be silent in some churches in order that pardons may be preached in others.

62. The true treasure of the church is the most holy gospel of the glory and grace of God.

THE EDWARDIAN HOMILIES

This document stems from the British Reformation and played a formative role in the Anglican Church. The Edwardian Homilies, or sermons, were written by Thomas Cranmer and were first published during the reign of Edward VI. The selection here is from the sermon on the Word of God, taken from *Certain Sermons or Homilies, Appointed to be read in churches in the time of the late Queen Elizabeth of famous memory* (Oxford: Oxford University Press, 1832).

Thomas Cranmer

A Fruitful Exhortation to the Reading and Knowledge of Holy Scripture

Unto a Christian man there can be nothing either more necessary or profitable, than the knowledge of holy scripture, forasmuch as in it is contained God's true word, setting forth his glory, and also man's duty. And there is no truth nor doctrine necessary for our justification and eternal salvation, but that is, or may be drawn out of that fountain and well of truth. Therefore as many as be desirous to enter into the right and perfect way of God, must apply their minds to know holy scripture; without the which, they can neither sufficiently know God and his will, neither their office and duty. And as drink is pleasant to them that be dry, and meat to them that be hungry; so is the reading, hearing, searching, and studying of holy scripture to them that be desirous to know God, or themselves, and to do his will. And their stomachs only do loathe and abhor the heavenly knowledge and food of God's word, that be so drowned in worldly vanities, that they neither savour God, nor any godliness: for that is the cause why they desire such vanities, rather than the true knowledge of God. . . .

The words of Holy Scripture be called words of everlasting life: for they be God's instrument, ordained for the same purpose. They have the power to convert through God's promise, and they be effectual through God's assistance, and (being received in a faithful heart) they have ever an heavenly spiritual working in them. . . . This word whoever is diligent to read, and in his heart to print that he readeth, the great affection to the transitory things of this world shall be diminished in him, and the great desire of heavenly things (that be therein promised of God) shall increase in him. And there is nothing that so much strengtheneth our faith and trust in God, that so much keepeth up innocency and pureness of the heart, and also of outward godly life and conversation, as continual reading and recording of God's word.

John Calvin

CALVIN'S *INSTITUTES*

The first edition of this classic theological text was published in 1535, just one year after Calvin's conversion to the faith. He revised and enlarged it throughout his life, the last edition coming off the press in 1559. Calvin structured the *Institutes* in four parts, taking his cue from the structure of the Apostles' Creed. The four parts or "books," as Calvin labels them, are the doctrines of God, Christ, the Holy Spirit, and the church. The two selections here are from book one, chapter two, point two (I.ii.2.) on the knowledge of God and book three, chapter twenty, point two (III.xx.2) on prayer. These excerpts are from the two-volume edition edited by John T. McNeill, translated and indexed by Ford Lewis Battles (Philadelphia: The Westminster Press, 1960), I:41-42; II:851.

Book One, Chapter Two, Point 2: *Knowledge of God Involves Trust and Reverence*

> What is God? Men who pose this question are merely toying with idle speculations. It is more important for us to know of what sort he is and what is consistent with his nature. What good is it to profess with Epicurus some sort of God who has cast aside the care of the world only to amuse himself in idleness? What help is it, in short, to know a God with whom we have nothing to do? Rather, our knowledge should serve first to teach us fear and reverence; secondly, with it as our guide and teacher, we should learn to seek every good from him, and, having received it, to credit it to his account. For how can the thought of God penetrate your mind without your realizing immediately that, since you are his handiwork, you have been made over and bound to his command by right of creation, that you owe your life to him?—that whatever you undertake, whatever you do, ought to be ascribed to him?

Book Three, Chapter Twenty, Point 2:
The Necessity of Prayer

> It is, therefore, by the benefit of prayer that we reach those riches which are laid up for us with the Heavenly Father. For there is a communion of men with God by which, having entered the heavenly sanctuary, they appeal to him in person concerning his promises in order to experience, where necessity so demands, that what they believed was not vain, although he had promised it in word alone. Therefore we see that to us nothing is promised to be expected from the Lord, which we are not also

bidden to ask of him in prayers. So true is that we dig up by prayer the treasures that were pointed out by the Lord's gospel, and which our faith has gazed upon.

Words fail to explain how necessary prayer is, and in how many ways the exercise of prayer is profitable. Surely, with good reason the Heavenly Father affirms that the only stronghold of safety is calling upon his name. By doing so we invoke the presence both of his providence, through which he watches over and guards our affairs, and of his power, through which he sustains us, weak as we are and well-nigh overcome, and of his goodness, through which he receives us, miserably burdened with sins, unto grace; and, in short, it is by prayer that we call him to reveal himself as wholly present to us. Hence comes an extraordinary peace and repose to our consciences. For having disclosed to the Lord the necessity that was pressing upon us, we even rest fully in the thought that none of our ills is hid from him who, we are convinced, has both the will and the power to take the best care of us.

CONFESSIONS OF
THE REFORMATION

The Reformation was rich in theological expression. All of the new denominations and churches needed to put their beliefs and commitments into writing. Many of these documents continue to have confessional status in denominations to this day.

THE SCHLEITHEIM CONFESSION

The earliest of the Reformation confessions, Schleitheim was largely the work of Michael Sattler and represents the Radical wing of the Reformation, or Anabaptism. It consists of seven articles. The sixth, on "the sword," is given here, taken from *The Doctrines of the Mennonites*, John C. Wenger, editor (Scottdale, PA: Herald Press, 1952).

Anabaptist Martyrdoms, Saltzburg, 1528

Sixth, we are agreed as follows concerning the sword: The sword is ordained of God outside the perfection of Christ. It punishes and puts to death the wicked, and guards and protects the good. In the Law the sword was ordained for the punishment of the wicked and for their death, and the same is now to be used by the worldly magistrates.

In the perfection of Christ, however, only the ban is used for a warning and for the excommunication of the one who has sinned, without putting the flesh to death—simply the warning and the command to sin no more.

Now it will be asked by many who do not recognize this as the will of Christ for us, whether a Christian may or should employ the sword against the wicked for the defense and protection of the good, or for the sake of love.

Our reply is unanimously as follows: Christ teaches and commands us to learn of him, for he is meek and lowly of heart and so shall we find rest to our souls. Also Christ says to the heathenish woman who was taken in adultery, not that one should stone her according to the law of his father (and yet he says, As the Father has commanded me, thus I do), but in mercy and forgiveness and warning, to sin no more. . . .

It will be asked concerning the sword, Shall one be a magistrate if one should be chosen as such? The answer is as follows: They wished to make Christ king, but he fled and did not view it as the arrangement of his Father. Thus shall we do as he did, and follow him, and so shall we not walk in darkness.

THE GENEVA CONFESSION, 1536

Largely the work of John Calvin, the first Geneva Confession (another one was produced in 1559) was adopted by the town authorities. A rather short document of only twenty-one chapters, this confession represents the thought of Calvin in outline. Chapters 7 and 18 are given here, taken from *Reformed Confessions of the Sixteenth Century*, Arthur C. Cochrane, editor (Louisville: Westminster John Knox Press, 2003), pages 121-122, 124-125.

7. Righteousness in Jesus

Therefore we acknowledge the things which are consequently given to us by God in Jesus Christ: the first, that being in our own natures enemies of God and subjects of his wrath and judgment, we are reconciled with him and received again in grace through the intercession of Jesus Christ, so that by his righteousness and guiltlessness we have remission of our sins, and by the shedding of his blood we are cleansed and purified from all our stains.

18. The Church

While there is only one Church of Jesus Christ, we always acknowledge that necessity requires companies of the faithful to be distributed in different places. Of these assemblies each one is called Church. But in as much as all companies do not assemble in the name of our Lord, but rather to blaspheme and pollute him by their unrighteous deeds, we believe that the proper mark by which rightly to discern the Church of Jesus Christ is that his holy gospel be purely and faithfully preached, proclaimed, heard, and kept, that his sacraments be properly administered, even if there be some imperfections and faults, as there always will be among men. On the other hand, where the gospel is not declared, heard, and received, there we do not acknowledge the form of the Church. Hence the churches governed by the ordinances of the pope are rather synagogues of the devil than Christian churches.

THE WESTMINSTER STANDARDS

A result of the work of the assembly convened from 1643 until 1649 by Parliament, the Westminster Standards include the Larger and Shorter Catechisms (1647), the Confession of Faith (1647), and the Directory for the Public Worship of God (1645). Selections here include Chapter 21 of the Confession and the beginning section on the preaching of the Word from the Directory, both selections underscoring the Puritan emphasis on the worship service and preaching.

The Westminster Confession of Faith, Chapter Twenty-One:
Of Religious Worship, and the Sabbath Day

1. The light of nature showeth that there is a God, who hath Lordship and Sovereignty over all, is good, and doth good unto all, and is therefore to be feared, loved, praised, called upon, trusted in, and served, with all the heart, with all the soul, and with all the might. But, the acceptable way of worshipping the true God, is instituted by himself, and so limited by his own revealed Will, that he may not be worshipped according to the imaginations and devices of men, or the suggestions of Satan, under any visible representation, or any other way not prescribed in the holy Scripture. . . .

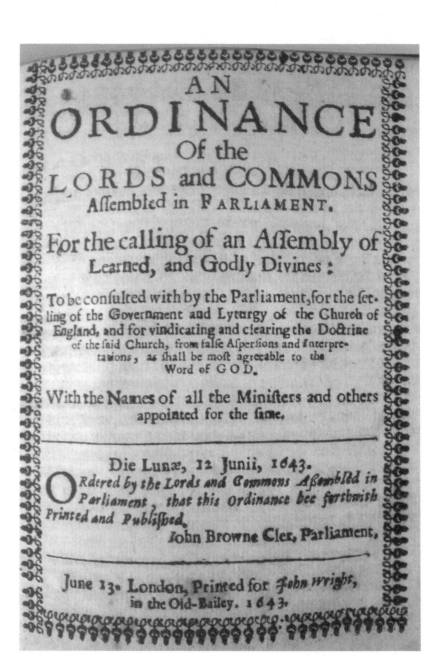

AN ORDINANCE
Of the
LORDS and COMMONS
Affembled in PARLIAMENT.

For the calling of an Affembly of Learned, and Godly Divines :

To be confulted with by the Parliament, for the fet-
ling of the Government and Lyturgy of the Church of
England, and for vindicating and clearing the Doctrine
of the faid Church, from falfe Afperfions and Interpre-
tations, as fhall be moft agreeable to the
Word of GOD.

With the Names of all the Minifters and others
appointed for the fame.

Die Lunæ, 12 Junii, 1643.

ORdered by the Lords and Commons Affembled in
Parliament, that this Ordinance bee forthwith
Printed and Publifhed.

John Browne Cler. Parliament.

June 13. London, Printed for *John Wright*,
in the Old-Bailey. 1643.

Ordinance by Parliament Calling for Westminster Assembly, 1643

140

7. As it is the law of nature, that, in general, a due proportion of time be set apart for the worship of God; so in his Word, by a positive, moral, and perpetual commandment, binding all men in all ages, he hath particularly appointed one day in seven for a Sabbath, to be kept holy unto him: which from the beginning of the world to the resurrection of Christ, was the last day of the week; and, from the resurrection of Christ, was changed into the first day of the week, which in Scripture is called the Lord's day, and is to be continued to the end of the world, as the Christian Sabbath.

8. This Sabbath is then kept holy unto the Lord, when men, after a due preparing of their hearts, and ordering of their common affairs beforehand, do not only observe a holy rest all the day from their own works, words, and thoughts, about their worldly employments and recreations; but also are taken up the whole time in the public and private exercises of his worship, and in the duties of necessity and mercy.

The Westminster Directory for the Public Worship of God, of the Preaching of the Word

Preaching of the Word, being the power of God unto salvation, and one of the greatest and most excellent works belonging to the ministry of the gospel, should be performed, that the workman need not be ashamed, but may save himself and those that hear him.

It is presupposed (according to the Rules for Ordination) that the minister of Christ is in some good measure gifted for so weighty a service, by his skill in the original languages (Hebrew and Greek), and in such arts and sciences as are handmaids unto divinity, by his knowledge in the whole body of theology, but most of all in the Holy Scriptures, having his senses and heart exercised in them above the common sort of believers; and by the illumination of God's Spirit, and other gifts of edification, which (together with reading and studying the Word) he ought still to seek by prayer, and a humble heart, resolving to admit and receive any truth not yet attained, whenever God shall make it known to him. All of which he is to make use of, and improve in his private preparations, before he deliver in public what he hath provided.

A
DIRECTORY
FOR

The Publique VVorſhip of *GOD*,

Throughout the Three

KINGDOMS
OF

England, Scotland, and *Ireland.*

Together with an Ordinance of Parliament for the taking away of the Book of

COMMON-PRAYER:
AND

For eſtabliſhing and obſerving of this preſent DIRECTORY
throughout the Kingdom of *England,* and Dominion of *Wales.*

Die Jovis, 13. *Martii,* 1644.

ORdered by the Lords and Commons aſſembled in Parliament, That this *Ordinance* and *Directory* bee forthwith Printed and Publiſhed:

Joh: Brown, Cleric.　　　　*H: Elſynge, Cler.*
Parliamentorum.　　　　　　*Parl.D.Com.*

LONDON:

Printed for *Evan Tyler, Alexander Fifield, Ralph Smith,* and *John Field* ; And are to be ſold at the Sign of the Bible in Cornhill, neer the ROYALL-EXCHANGE. 1644.

Directory for Public Worship, 1644

CATECHISMS OF THE REFORMATION

A catechism is a teaching tool. You might recognize the English word *echo* in the middle of it. A teacher asks a pupil a question, who gives back the question with an answer. The catechisms of the Reformation were used to train the next generation in the faith and for times of family worship. Luther, who wrote his *Large Catechism*, sometimes called the *German Catechism*, for the training of ministers and his *Small Catechism*, sometimes called *Children's Catechism*, for children had this to say about catechisms and the doctrines of the church:

> We cannot perpetuate these and other teachings unless we train the people who come after us and succeed us in our office and work, so that they in turn may bring up their children successfully. Thus the Word of God and the Christian Church will be preserved. Therefore let every head of a household remember that it is his duty, by God's injunction and command, to teach or to have taught to his children the things they ought to know.

LUTHER'S *LARGE CATECHISM* (1529), ON THE LORD'S SUPPER

Luther intended this catechism as a training tool for ministers in the basics of theology. The selection that follows concerns his understanding of the Lord's Supper.

> The Lord's Supper is given as a daily food and sustenance so that our faith may refresh and strengthen itself and not weaken in the struggle but grow continually stronger. For the new life should be one that continually develops and progresses. Meanwhile it must suffer much opposition. The devil is a furious enemy; when he sees that we resist him and attack the old man, and when he cannot rout us by force, he sneaks and skulks about everywhere, trying all kinds of tricks, and does not stop until he has finally

worn us out so that we either renounce our faith or yield hand and foot and become indifferent or impatient. For such times, when our heart feels too sorely oppressed, this comfort of the Lord's Supper is given to bring us new strength and refreshment.

THE HEIDELBERG CATECHISM (1563)

Representing the Swiss Reformation, this catechism begins with perhaps the finest piece of theological writing of all time. The catechism, primarily written by Zacharias Ursinus and Caspar Olevianus, proceeds in three parts, unfolding the three things that we need to know: the greatness of our sin and misery, the redemption provided through Christ's work on the cross, and the response of living a life of gratitude to God for his work in redemption.

Caspar Olevianus

Question 1: What is thy only comfort in life and in death?

Answer: That I, with body and soul, both in life and in death, am not my own, but belong to my faithful Savior Jesus Christ, who with his precious blood has fully satisfied for all my sins, and redeemed me from all the power of the devil; and so preserves me that without the will of my Father in heaven not a hair can fall from my head; yea, that all things must work together for my salvation. Wherefore, by his Holy Spirit, he also assures me of eternal life, and makes me heartily willing and ready henceforth to live unto him.

Question 2: How many things are necessary for thee to know that thou in this comfort mayest live and die happily?

Answer: Three things: First, the greatness of my sin and misery. Second, how I am redeemed from all my sins and misery. Third, how I am to be thankful to God for such redemption.

THE WESTMINSTER SHORTER CATECHISM (1647)

The first question and answer of *The Westminster Shorter Catechism* is as equally stirring as that of the *Heidelberg Catechism*, just more concise. Below follows the famous first question, the next two on Scripture, and the Catechism's discussion of the work of Christ in his threefold office (*munis triplex*) of Prophet, Priest, and King.

Question 1: What is the chief end of man?

Answer: Man's chief end is to glorify God, and to enjoy him forever.

Question 2: What rule hath God given to direct us how we may glorify and enjoy him?

Answer: The Word of God, which is contained in the Scriptures of the Old and New Testaments, is the only rule to direct us how we may glorify and enjoy him.

Question 3: What do the Scriptures principally teach?

Answer: The Scriptures principally teach what man is to believe concerning God, and what duty God requires of man.

Question 23: What offices doth Christ execute as our Redeemer?

Answer: Christ, as our redeemer, executes the offices of a Prophet, of a Priest, and of a King, both in his state of humiliation and exaltation.

Question 24: How doth Christ execute the office of a Prophet?

Answer: Christ executes the office of a Prophet, in revealing to us by his Word and Spirit, the will of God for our salvation.

Question 25: How doth Christ execute the office of a Priest?

Answer: Christ executes the office of a Priest, in his once offering up of himself a sacrifice to satisfy divine justice, and reconcile us to God, and in making continual intercession for us.

Question 26: How doth Christ execute the office of a King?

Answer: Christ executes the office of a King, in subduing us to himself, in ruling and defending us, and in restraining and conquering all his and our enemies.

PRAYERS OF
THE REFORMATION

The Reformation witnessed reforms across the board, encompassing preaching, theology, missions and evangelism, and piety and
personal devotion. The written prayers from that era testify to the
depth of spirituality of the Reformers and are among the best Reformation
literature.

THE BOOK OF COMMON PRAYER

The Book of Common Prayer contains the liturgy for services in the
Anglican Church as well as prayers for special occasions. It is a sort
of guidebook for the Christian's worship and life. Some of the prayers
for the church service are recited by the priest; others are responsive
prayers including the congregation. One such prayer for the morning
follows. Included here are also prayers for going to sea and for storms at
sea. Taken from *The Book of Common Prayer* (Oxford: Oxford University
Press), pages 49, 619-620.

Morning Prayer

Priest. O Lord, show thy mercy upon us.
Answer. And grant us thy salvation.
Priest. O Lord, save the Queen.
Answer. And mercifully hear us when we call upon thee.
Priest. Endue thy ministers with righteousness.
Answer. And make thy chosen people joyful.
Priest. O Lord, save thy people.
Answer. And bless thine inheritance.
Priest. Give peace in our time, O Lord.
Answer. Because there is none other that fighteth for us, but only thou, O God.
Priest. O God, make clean our hearts within us.
Answer. And take not thy Holy Spirit from us.

Prayer to Be Used at Sea

O Eternal Lord God, who alone spreadest out the heavens, and rulest the raging of the sea; who hast compassed the waters with bounds until day and night come to an end. Be pleased to receive into thy Almighty and most gracious protection the persons of us thy servants, and the Fleet in which we serve. Preserve us from the dangers of the sea, and from the violence of the enemy; that we may be a safeguard unto our most gracious Sovereign Lady, Queen Elizabeth, and her Dominions, and a security for such as pass on the seas upon their lawful occasions; that the inhabitants of our Island may in peace and quietness serve thee our God; and that we may return in safety to enjoy the blessings of the land, with the fruits of our labors, and with a thankful remembrance of thy mercies to praise and glorify thy holy Name; through Jesus Christ our Lord. Amen.

Short Prayer in Respect of a Storm at Sea

Thou, O Lord, that stillest the raging of the sea, hear, hear us, and save us, that we perish not.
O blessed Saviour, that didst save thy disciples ready to perish in a storm, hear us, and save us, we beseech thee.
Lord, have mercy upon us.
Christ, have mercy upon us.
Lord, have mercy upon us.
O Lord, hear us.
O Christ, hear us.
God the Father, God the Son, God the Holy Ghost, have mercy upon us, save us now and evermore. Amen.

EVENING PRAYER OF JOHN CALVIN

John Calvin wrote a number of prayers for various occasions. His catechism of 1642 included a morning and evening prayer. The latter follows.

Lord God, since thou hast made the night for man to rest as thou hast created the day for his work, I beseech thee to give my body a restful night and to grant that my soul may be lifted up to thee and my heart always filled with thy love.

Teach me, O God, to entrust all my cares to thee and constantly remember thy mercy, so that my soul may enjoy spiritual rest. Let not my sleep be excessive, but let it serve to renew my strength so that I may be more ready to serve thee. May it please thee also to keep me pure in body and in spirit, preserving me from all temptations and all danger, so that my very sleep may contribute to the glory of thy name.

And since this day has not passed without my offending thee in several ways, I who am a poor sinner make this request. Grant, O God, that just as now thou hast hid all things in the shadows of the night, thou wilt also bury all my sins in thy mercy, through Jesus Christ my Savior. Amen.

A PRAYER OF RICHARD SIBBES

Representing Puritan prayers, written for their own devotion and for their congregations, Richard Sibbes (1577–1635) offers this short but comprehensive prayer. Taken from Howard L. Rice and Lamar Williamson, Jr., editors, *A Book of Reformed Prayers* (Louisville: Westminster John Knox Press, 1998), page 32.

Lord, Thou hast made Thyself to be ours, therefore now show Thyself to us in Thy wisdom, goodness, and power. To walk faithfully in our Christian course we need much grace. Supply us out of Thy rich store. We need wisdom to go in and out inoffensively before others; furnish us with Thy Spirit. We need patience and comfort. Thou that art the God of consolation bestow it upon us; for Christ's sake. Amen.

A PRAYER OF ANNE BRADSTREET

America's first poet, Anne Bradstreet (1612–1672) artfully reflects Puritan thought in her poems. This poem is a prayer on behalf of her oldest son Samuel as he set off on a voyage to England. Taken from Heidi L. Nichols, *Anne Bradstreet: A Guided Tour of the Life and Thought of a Puritan Poet* (Phillipsburg, NJ: P&R, 2006), page 133.

Upon my Son Samuel his goeing for England, Novem. 6, 1657.

Thou mighty God of Sea and Land,
I here resigne into thy hand
The Son of Prayers, of vowes, of teares,
The child I stay'd for many yeares.
Thou heard'st me then, and gav'st him me;
Hear me again, I give him Thee.
He's mine, but more, O Lord, Thine own,
For sure thy Grace on him is shone.

No friend I have like Thee to trust,
For mortall helpes are brittle Dust.
Preserve, O Lord, from stormes and wrack,
Protect him there, and bring him back;
And if thou shalt spare me a space,
That I again may see his face,
Then shall I celebrate thy Praise,
And Bless thee for't even all my Dayes.
If otherwise I goe to Rest,
Thy Will bee done, for that is best;
Perswade my heart I shall him see
For ever happefy'd with Thee.

NOTES

CHAPTER ONE:
FIVE HUNDRED YEARS OLD AND STILL GOING STRONG:
WHY THE REFORMATION MATTERS TODAY

1. Mark A. Noll and Carolyn Nystrom, *Is The Reformation Over? An Evangelical Assessment of Contemporary Roman Catholicism* (Grand Rapids, MI: Baker Academic, 2005).

2. "Evangelicals and Catholics Together," *First Things* 43 (May 1994), 15-22.

3. See various documents related to the Anglican-Roman Catholic International Commission (ARCIC), such as "The Agreed Statement on Eucharistic Doctrine" and "Agreed Statements on Authority in the Church," available online at www.prounione.urbe.it.

CHAPTER TWO:
A MONK AND A MALLET: MARTIN LUTHER AND
THE GERMAN REFORMATION

1. Portions of this chapter are reprinted from Stephen J. Nichols, "Luther and the Reformation," *New Horizons* (26:9), October 2005, 3-4.

2. For a fuller discussion of Luther, see Stephen J. Nichols, *Martin Luther: A Guided Tour of His Life and Thought* (Philipsburg, NJ: P&R, 2002).

3. For further discussion and a complete text of the Ninety-Five Theses, see Stephen J. Nichols, ed., *Martin Luther's Ninety-Five Theses* (Phillipsburg, NJ: P&R, 2002).

4. Ibid., 35-37, 39.

5. For a fuller treatment of the Reformation *Solas*, see James Montgomery Boice, *Whatever Happened to the Gospel of Grace? Rediscovering the Doctrines That Shook the World* (Wheaton, IL: Crossway Books, 2001).

6. See his sermon by that title in the book *No Little People* (Wheaton, IL: Crossway Books, 2003).

7. For more on Luther and Katy, as well as more on Luther and marriage, see the essay by Justin Taylor, "Martin Luther's Reform of Marriage," in *Sex and the Supremacy of Christ*, ed. John Piper and Justin Taylor (Wheaton, IL: Crossway Books, 2005), 213-244.

8. *Martin Luther* (1953) was directed by Irving Pichel and starred Niall McGinnis. It garnered two Oscar nominations. In 2003 MGM released *Luther*, directed by Eric Till and starring Joseph Fiennes.

9. See Luther's *Table Talk*, Nos. 122 and 5418. His Table Talks were accounts of Luther's interaction with his family, colleagues, and students around his dinner table. Students began recording these exchanges in 1531 and continued until his death. As a unique historical document, *Table Talk* provides an intriguing window into Luther behind the scenes.

10. *Table Talk*, No. 547.

11. *Table Talk*, Nos. 2849b and 1348.

12. *Table Talk*, No. 5239.

CHAPTER THREE:
SOME MIDDLE-AGED MEN AND A SAUSAGE SUPPER: ULRICH ZWINGLI AND THE SWISS REFORMATION

1. The sermon is reprinted in *The Works of Zwingli: Volume One, 1510–1522*, ed. Samuel Macauley Jackson (New York: G. P. Putnam, 1912), 70-112.

2. For a full biography of Zwingli, see G. R. Potter, *Zwingli* (Cambridge: Cambridge University Press, 1976).

3. See Roland A. Bainton, *Erasmus of Christendom* (New York: Scribner's, 1969), 129-150.

4. *The Works of Zwingli: Volume One, 1510–1522*, 150-165. The Latin word is *conniveat*, which literally means "to wink."

5. Ulrich Zwingli, "Of the Clarity and Certainty of the Word of God," in *Zwingli and Bullinger*, Library of Christian Classics, Vol. 24, ed. G. W. Bromiley (Philadelphia: Westminster Press, 1953), 59-95.

6. The term *transubstantiation* comes from the Latin. When the priest pronounced, "This is my body," the wafer would cross over (*trans*) and become a new *substance*, literally becoming the body of Christ. Likewise the wine became his blood, it was believed.

7. For more on Luther and Zwingli on the Lord's Supper, see Stephen J. Nichols, *Martin Luther: A Guided Tour of His Life and Thought* (Phillipsburg, NJ: P&R, 2002), 117-130.

CHAPTER FOUR:
THE NOT-SO-RADICAL RADICAL REFORMERS:
THE ANABAPTISTS AND THE REFORMATION

1. The most severe law came in 592. The Code of Justinian made non-infant baptism, along with heresies related to the doctrine of the Trinity, punishable by death.

2. Both the Schleitheim and Dordrecht Confessions may be found in *Creeds of the Churches: A Reader in Christian Doctrine from the Bible to the Present*, third edition, ed. John H. Leith (Louisville: Westminster John Knox Press, 1982), 281-308.

3. See Martin Luther, *The Large Catechism* (Philadelphia: Fortress Press, 1959), 2-5.

4. An account of the trial and martyrdom is recorded in Thieleman J. van Braght, *Martyrs Mirror* (Scottdale, PA: Herald Press, 1938, reprint 2002), 416-420.

5. Ibid., 420.

6. See *The Complete Writings of Menno Simons*, ed. J. C. Wenger (Scottdale, PA: Herald Press, 1956).

7. H. Richard Niebuhr, *Christ & Culture* (New York: Harper, 1951, reprint 2001).

8. For a contemporary perspective espousing a similar view, see John Howard Yoder, *The Politics of Jesus*, second edition (Grand Rapids, MI: Eerdmans, 1994).

9. See John Hostetter, *Amish Society*, fourth edition (Baltimore: Johns Hopkins University Press, 1993).

CHAPTER FIVE:
AN OVERNIGHT STAY IN GENEVA:
JOHN CALVIN AND THE SWISS REFORMATION

1. For a fuller biography, see Alister E. McGrath, *A Life of John Calvin* (Oxford: Blackwell, 1990).

2. See Stephen J. Nichols, *Pages from Church History: A Guided Tour of Christian Classics* (Phillipsburg, NJ: P&R, 2006) for a discussion of Calvin and *The Institutes*.

3. John Calvin, *Institutes*, Book IV, Chapter 1.1.

4. John Calvin to Martin Luther, January 21, 1545, in *Calvin's Selected Works*, Vol. 4: *Letters, Part 1, 1528–1545*, ed. Jules Bonnet and David Constable (Grand Rapids, MI: Baker, 1983), 442.

5. John Calvin, *Golden Booklet of the True Christian Life*, trans. Henry J. Van Andel (Grand Rapids, MI: Baker, 1952), 22.

CHAPTER SIX:
A KING AND A DIVORCE: THE ANGLICANS AND
THE BRITISH REFORMATION

1. John H. Leith, ed., *Creeds of the Churches* (Louisville: John Knox Press, 1982), 244.

CHAPTER SEVEN:
MEN IN BLACK: THE PURITANS AND
THE BRITISH REFORMATION

1. For more on Edwards and his sermons, see Stephen J. Nichols, *Jonathan Edwards: A Guided Tour of His Life and Thought* (Phillipsburg, NJ: P&R, 2001).

2. See Stephen J. Nichols, *Pages from Church History: A Guided Tour of Christian Classics* (Phillipsburg, NJ: P&R, 2006).

3. There were suspicions that Charles II was a closet Roman Catholic. His wife was Catholic and had a great influence on him in that direction.

4. William Ames, *The Marrow of Theology*, trans. John Dykstra Eusden (Grand Rapids, MI: Baker, 1997).

5. For an overview of some of the best Puritan texts, see Kelly M. Kapic and Randall C. Gleason, eds., *The Devoted Life: An Invitation to the Puritan Classics* (Downers Grove, IL: InterVarsity Press, 2004).

6. See J. I. Packer, *The Quest for Godliness: The Puritan Vision of the Christian Life* (Wheaton, IL: Crossway Books, 1994) and Leland Ryken, *Worldly Saints: The Puritans as They Really Were* (Grand Rapids, MI: Zondervan, 1986).

7. Jeremiah Burroughs, *The Rare Jewel of Christian Commitment* (Carlisle, PA: The Banner of Truth Trust, 2001), 19, 83.

8. For discussions of all the Puritans listed here, see Kapic and Gleason, eds., *The Devoted Life: An Invitation to the Puritan Classics*.

9. A. G. Dickens, *The English Reformation*, second edition (University Park, PA: The Pennsylvania State University Press, 1989), 376 and Patrick Collinson, *The Reformation: A History* (New York: The Modern Library, 2004), 138.

CHAPTER EIGHT:
WOMEN IN BLACK TOO: THE UNTOLD STORY OF WOMEN AND THE REFORMATION

1. Edwin Woodruff Tait, "Bride of the Reformation," *Christian History*, October 2004.

2. Cited in Roland Bainton, *Women of the Reformation in Germany and Italy* (Minneapolis: Augsburg, 1971), 82. Wibrandis and Oecolampadius had three children—Eusebius, who died at the age of thirteen, Alatheia, and Irene.

3. I am grateful to one of my students, Jessica Radcliffe, for her research on Katherine Zell.

4. The letters to Viret and Farel may be found in *Calvin's Selected Works, Vol. 5: Letters Part 2, 1545–1558*, ed. Jules Bonnet and David Constable (Grand Rapids, MI: Baker, 1983), 216-219.

5. Citations in Rudolf K. Markwald and Marilynn Morris Markwald, *Katharina Von Bora: A Reformation Life* (St. Louis: Concordia, 2002), 176, 192-193.

6. Cited in *Voices of the English Reformation, A Sourcebook*, ed. John N. King (Philadelphia: University of Pennsylvania Press, 2004), 320.

7. Cited in Paul F. M. Zahl, *Five Women of the English Reformation* (Grand Rapids, MI: Eerdmans, 2001), 109-113.

8. Cited in *Voices of the English Reformation*, 324.

9. *Calvin's Selected Works: Letters*, Vol. 7, 162.

10. Roland Bainton, *Women of the Reformation in France and England* (Minneapolis: Augsburg, 1973), 38.

11. The estimates by contemporaries and historians vary, some placing it as low as five thousand, others as high as thirty thousand.

12. Cited in Nancy Lyman Roelker, *Queen of Navarre: Jeanne d'Albert, 1528–1572* (Cambridge, MA: Harvard University Press, 1968), 340.

13. Heidi L. Nichols, *Anne Bradstreet: A Guided Tour of the Life and Thought of a Puritan Poet* (Phillipsburg, NJ: P&R, 2006), 196.

14. Ibid., 186.

15. Ibid., 189.
16. Cited in *Women Writers of the Reformation*, 311.
17. Cited in Bainton, *Women of the Reformation in France and England*, 21.
18. See Steven Ozment, *When Fathers Ruled: Family Life in Reformation Europe* (Cambridge, MA: Harvard University Press, 1983) and Lyndal Roper, *The Holy Household: Women and Morals in Reformation Augsburg* (Oxford: Oxford University Press, 1989).

Please visit
www.monkandamallet.com

REFORMATION

	CHAPTER 2 The Reformation in Germany	CHAPTER 3 The Reformation in Zurich	CHAPTER 4 The Radical Reformation
KEY PLAYERS	Martin Luther Philip Melanchthon Frederick the Wise	Ulrich Zwingli Heinrich Bullinger	Conrad Grebel Michael Sattler Menno Simons
MAJOR EVENTS	Posting of Ninety-Five Theses, October 31, 1517 Diet of Worms, 1521	Sausage supper, 1522 1st & 2nd Disputation, 1523	Baptism of George Blaurock, 1525 Persecution and martyrdoms, 1525-1618
SIGNIFICANT TEXTS	Ninety-Five Theses German Bible Augsburg Confession	Erasmus's Greek New Testament Zwingli's *The True and False Religion*	Schleitheim Confession *Martyrs Mirror*
LEGACY	Protestantism Lutheranism	The Reformed Church	Anabaptism Mennonites Amish

SCORECARD

CHAPTER 5	CHAPTER 6	CHAPTER 7	CHAPTER 8
The Reformation in Geneva	The Reformation in Britain, Part 1: Anglicanism	The Reformation in Britain, Part 2: Puritanism	Women of the Reformation
John Calvin	Henry VIII	Oliver Cromwell	Katherina von Bora
Theodore Beza	Thomas Cranmer	John Bunyan	Lady Jane Grey
	John Knox	Jeremiah Burroughs	Queen Jeanne of Navarre
			Anne Bradstreet
Calvin arrives in Geneva, 1536	Act of Supremacy, 1534	Acts of Conformity, 1559-1564	Marriage of Katherina Von Bora and Martin Luther, 1525
Synod of Dort, 1618-1619	English Bible, 1525-1611	British Civil War, 1640s	Jane Grey's attempt at the throne, 1553
	Reign of Bloody Mary, 1553-1558	Act of Toleration, 1689	St. Bartholomew's Day Massacre, 1572
Calvin's *Institutes of the Christian Religion*	*The Book of Common Prayer & The Homilies*	Westminster Standards	Letters of Queen Jeanne of Navarre
Canons of the Synod of Dort	Thirty-Nine Articles	Bunyan's *Pilgrim's Progress*	Bradstreet's *Tenth Muse*
The Reformed Church	Anglicanism	Presbyterianism	The parsonage
Presbyterianism	Methodism (later development)	Congregationalism (Independents)	Family life
		Baptists